More Than Seventy Summers

MORE THAN
SEVENTY SUMMERS

Tony Harman and Ruth Boyd

with illustrations by
Lyn O'Neill

WHITTET BOOKS

First published 1990
Text © 1990 by Tony Harman and Ruth Boyd
Illustrations © 1990 by Lyn O'Neill
Whittet Books Ltd, 18 Anley Road, London W14 0BY

Many of these pieces were the result of Tony Harman starting, at the age of
seventy, to write for the *Guardian*, and have appeared in that paper.

Design by Paul Minns

Typesetting by Litho Link Limited, Welshpool, Powys, Wales

Printing and binding by Biddles of Guildford

British Library Cataloguing in Publication Data
Harman, Tony
 More than seventy summers.
 1. Buckinghamshire. Chesham. Agriculture, history
 I. Title II. Boyd, Ruth
 630'.92'4

ISBN 0-905483-81-2

CONTENTS

. . . we spend our years as a tale that is told. The days of our years are threescore years and ten; and if by reason of strength they be fourscore years, yet is their strength labour and sorrow; for it is soon cut off, and we fly away . . .

PSALM 90

To feel the sun . . .
And not to see the flowers.
The wind . . .
And not the waving corn.
Is just the labour and the sorrow,
Because, by reason of my strength
I have lived for more than threescore years and ten.
And yet, the world's still there.
Still beautiful the way it always was,
And many people in it whom I love.
So much is lost and yet a lot remains.
So, I still want a year or two
Of aching limbs and straining eyes . . .
But not the seventy more I sought five years ago.

T.H.

Is it the sentiments of King David all those thousands of years ago, or the language of Reformation England, that makes it seem so right for me?

IT's All Still There

We are all affected by nostalgia. Perhaps it is because most of us liked being young that we feel things must have been better then? And, if they were better then, long ago they must have been better still. It is a human weakness to sentimentalize the past — to remember what has gone and to fail to appreciate the here and now.

The picture of the world as it was in previous generations can still be traced on the landscape. Changes in agriculture alter the look of the countryside but do not necessarily spoil it. The open-field system of the Middle Ages was not particularly beautiful, rather bare, plain, with no hedges; forests in the distance, but no woods in the fields. The hedges and small woods which heighten our landscape have all come since, as a result of the changing patterns of agriculture. Even some commercial and industrial developments in time produce a beauty of their own — the canals, reservoirs, man-made lakes.

Man does not always destroy the beauties of nature, and nature is much stronger than we realize. The roadside verges of motorways are havens for wild life. And when, during the war, buildings of London were demolished by bombs, in no time at all the sites were covered by wild flowers. Some were blown in by the wind or carried by birds, but others came from the seeds of plants that had been there long ago, perhaps before the buildings were even built. They had been waiting all the time to spring into life when they were given half a chance.

It's the same with woodland. It is terrible to see the clear-felling of a wood one has known all one's life. But, when it is done, nature takes over and other plants appear. I was there when my father cut down a wood on our land in 1920. Foxgloves sprang up from the seeds of those that had grown there before the wood had ever been planted, a hundred years before. Then the trees that grew naturally on the site, or that I subsequently planted, themselves grew large and killed the foxgloves — or so it seemed. Many years later, I clear-felled the wood again. Next year the foxgloves were back, springing up from the seed that had been left behind in my father's time.

The worst things we have done to our environment were inflicted when we were hungry and had to give first consideration to survival. The peasants of Brazil destroy the rain forests — with potentially catastrophic results for the rest of the world — because they are paid by the landowners to cut them down; then they can buy food. When the forest is cleared, food can be grown. They do not wish to destroy a basic asset of the whole world, but they want to eat. In an exact parallel, thousands of years ago, the population of Europe destroyed its original forests in order to grow food to survive.

But, when his belly is full, man thinks beyond simply utilizing his environment for his own needs. Conscience seems to be the main factor that singles him out from other animals. Or perhaps it is consciousness? It is curious that, as soon as our stomachs are filled, we become consumed by apprehension and guilt. The western world having, through science, solved the problem of producing enough food — but not the problem of how to distribute it to more needy countries — becomes increasingly obsessed by threats to his environment and to other species of animals. We are concerned with the need to preserve other species even when they are the natural enemies of man.

The fox doesn't deliberately leave a stock of rabbits to breed him food for next year; he just doesn't happen to catch them as fast as they breed. The crow doesn't deliberately leave the eggs in some bird's nest, he just can't find them all; so the other birds that are his prey continue to exist. Maybe man's difference stems, in part, from the fact that he has always imposed his will over other animals and made them breed as he wishes. Certainly, when he has enough to eat, he considers, in varying degrees, the rights of other species to exist and also the effects of his actions on the future of the world. Which is as well; that way we can avoid disaster.

Through awareness of what he has done, man can put right the damage he has caused. It has become fashionable to be a prophet of doom, to be negative about our surroundings; but all the environmental problems we face can be dealt with, without minimizing them. And the beauty of the world is still there, all around us, just as it has always been if we look for it and encourage it. It has not all gone. Give it a chance. We can enjoy nostalgia but still appreciate the world as it is now.

ALL CHANGE

The first men to come to this area, thousands of years ago, settled on the eastern edge of Chesham, just under a steep hill; so steep it was almost like a cliff. From where they lived, they had the most beautiful view. Set out before them were several little valleys joining together, green and full of trees and shrubs. Only about a hundred yards or so away two or three little streams had joined together to form a bright, clean, unpolluted river. On the hills behind and in front of them, and everywhere they looked, were great trees: a forest full of wildlife, birds and flowers. They didn't need to think about altering their environment and destroying the scenery. There were fish in the river and game in the forests and nuts and berries at some times of the year, so that as long as there weren't very many people they could live well and didn't need to change anything.

Later on more men came and probably there wasn't enough fish and game to go round. In any case, some of the new people were different. They had discovered that you could alter nature and turn it to your own use, that you could make the sort of things grow which you could eat, and make animals work for you. As the population grew, they were often hungry and they wished that the big trees were not there on the best land so that it would be easier to clear and grow better crops. The wild animals and the birds preyed upon the crops so that they didn't even get all that they had grown, and the wild flowers spread and there were weeds in their crops. So they started to slash and burn smaller trees and clear them so that they could grow more crops. They slashed and burnt just to get the trees out of their way, not because they needed the timber.

Where the country was not covered with forest, it was bog and marsh or open moorland downs or sometimes barren mountains, each of these teeming with its own special wildlife, its own special flowers and plants, its own special animals and birds. So the forest had to be cleared, the bog and marsh drained, the moorlands so far as possible cleared of stones and the stones used to divide them up into enclosures to keep the livestock in.

They had to try to create the best possible conditions for producing food — land as level as possible, well drained, free of obstruction and in enclosures suitable for the power unit that they had at the time. Since man himself was the power unit, he had to start the cultivation in small strips; the power unit decides the size of the enclosure. Every time any of these things were done, the wildlife was destroyed or at least disturbed and altered, all to feed people. The mountain tops alone could not be altered. Much later on, after the ground had been cleared, other problems appeared. Acid soils had to be treated with lime to make them neutral, if not alkaline, and in some cases after the trees had gone, light soil would blow away so clay had to be applied. In other cases, hedges and plantations had to be re-planted to stop the blowing. So in those areas new species of plants and birds established themselves in the hedges and shelter belts or perhaps old species re-established themselves.

Everybody is talking about conservation and protecting the environment and our inheritance. What do they mean by it? Do they mean freezing it in exactly the state it was when they first saw it? Anybody interested would be well advised to get the very first 6 inch Ordnance Survey map that was ever printed as a result of surveys done around 1877.

Looking at the map of where I live as it was a hundred years ago, I was struck with how beautiful it must have been — few houses, small fields, hedges, trees everywhere and, around every corner, a pond or chalk pit or some interesting feature; and now it is nearly all gone. Then, when I looked into it further, I realized that it was I who, in the last fifty years or so, had swept many of these features away. I remember that, when I was doing it, I was congratulated by all and sundry for increasing food production. When I filled in the dells and ponds, I had a perfectly good conscience because, then, people were saying, 'Produce as much food as you can.' I did it at a good time. Those who are doing it now get a lot of stick. Looking at that map makes me feel fairly remorseful.

What has changed, and why? The countryside has become suburbs. The landscape has altered because of changes in farming. First of all, there was arable farming and then there was stock farming. Now, it is back to arable farming. Self-sufficiency in the countryside has gone and has been replaced by total dependence upon the outside world. Great variety has changed to total specialization. Rural slums have become period cottages for stockbrokers and the population, which was stable for many years, has been dispersed and gone to the towns.

Of course, changes have always taken place. The countryside, which has opened out with the creation of larger farms and the final change-over to mechanized arable farming, had changed in the opposite direction before, continually opening up and then closing down again. When the original forests were cleared, it was opened up. Then, when the hedges were planted and the commons enclosed, it became closed up again. Every time a landowner planted a wood or shelter belt in the interest of sport, it closed in a little. Every time anybody planted an orchard, it closed in and every time anybody changed their methods and took the orchard out or felled the wood for timber, it opened up a bit. So, there is nothing new, just that the process has speeded up. Previously, it was almost like a long-term rotation. Now it is not; it is a fixed pattern which will probably stay.

All the time, good farmers, in the sense of farmers who produce a lot of food, tend to spoil the scenery and bad farmers tend to improve it by letting parts of it get overgrown. All during the 'twenties and 'thirties hedgerow trees were felled and sold for timber because farmers needed money, but they grew up again because farmers could not afford to keep the hedges cut. It is pretty well axiomatic that the greater the production of food, the less interesting the scenery. So nobody spoils the scenery for any reason other than that he wishes to do his job better according to his lights. Even somebody like Hugh Batchelor, who attracted a lot of publicity by getting into trouble for felling trees, is only an extreme example of a man who, by conventional standards, is a good farmer, doing what seems logical to him but, of course, going much too far.

In the same way, it could be said that good local authorities tend to spoil the countryside. They straighten the roads and make them wider to save people's lives, but it does not look as nice as romantic winding lanes, inconvenient though they may have been. There are few green lanes nowadays.

Unproductive though farming was sixty years ago, it still employed a great number of people and, even in the depths of the Depression in the 'twenties and 'thirties, there were three or four times as many people working on the local farms as there are now — producing very little, which of course is the reason why their standard of life was very low. Most of them had little or no alternative without going into the local towns to work and most of them came from families which had been on that particular land for a long time. The normal thing, when you got married, was to go to work on the same farm as your family or on one of the neighbouring ones.

None of the ordinary working people owned anything much at all. Unlike the French peasant, who had a large garden and usually owned his own house, thanks to Napoleon, nobody had much security in the Buckinghamshire countryside. In practice, they did not often have to move houses and rarely lost their jobs, but they were entirely dependent upon their employers for their houses. It cannot have been a comfortable situation. You can understand resentment about the tied-cottage system even if, in practice, hardly any evictions ever took place.

Rural industries have almost entirely disappeared. The blacksmith has gone, because the type of machinery on the farm is now so different. Perhaps many people don't know that the blacksmith's main job was repairing machinery, rather than shoeing horses. He used to repair the old, simple machines and, in some cases, even make them. Big, complicated machines now are really not readily repairable. They have built-in obsolescence and are changed by farmers very frequently. On Grove Farm we were using a corn drill in 1940 which had been bought second-hand thirty years before and was still running, repaired every year at the blacksmith's. Now, we have a completely new corn drill roughly every eight to ten years and the old one would be utterly useless, rusted away by the chemicals sown with the seed and shaken to bits by the speed at which it is run by the tractor.

The variety has gone out of farming because of the need to specialize in order to produce food cheap enough for the townsman to buy. Poultry, running around the farmyard picking up scraps, did not lay very many eggs, so the eggs were expensive. Hens kept in cages or in deep-litter houses, with artificial light to make them work long hours, produce a lot of eggs. So there are no longer any hens on the farm; instead they live in factories, because the urban population has insisted upon their eggs being cheap. To a limited extent, the same thing applies to pigs and vegetables.

Because townsmen want cheap food the countryman is driven all the while to think about new methods and adopt them if they seem to apply — new breeds of plants, new breeds of cattle. And the process is accelerating. The cost in terms of man-hours of home-produced food now is much less than it was half a century ago. At the same time, the people who are producing the food are enjoying a much higher standard of living, which is a measure of the technical change which in itself has spoiled the countryside. Only where there are large rich estates has there at any time been any planning of the countryside for its appearance sake. All of it has been purely a by-product of methods of agriculture. If you have small farms with people with a lower standard of life, you will get small fields and small herds of livestock. If you have large farms with people with a high standard of life, you will get large fields and the use of every possible mechanical means within them.

During the period, there has been an enormous change in wildlife. It is not all a question of the number of wild animals and birds being reduced, more a change in their distribution. There are far more badgers in this Chiltern area than there have probably been in history. It is not quite clear why. There are also far more foxes, although fox-hunting still goes on. In fact, there are so many foxes that, even supposing poultry could economically be kept running around farmyards, they would not last long in most situations. Rabbits have not been diminished very much by farming operations, just by myxomatosis. There are now several sorts of deer, whereas sixty years ago there were practically no deer at all.

As far as birds are concerned, there are fewer partridges and fewer pheasants, possibly because there are no gamekeepers to look after them. There are fewer thrushes and blackbirds because the hedges have been taken out. There are far more skylarks — probably because they live in open fields and fields are now more open — and just as many of the smaller birds, like yellow-hammers. The attractive, larger birds, like the woodpeckers, still abound in the woods. Owls have been reduced and hawks seem to have increased. Somebody must know why. Magpies have certainly increased and ought to be reduced since they prey on the small birds. There seem to be far fewer plover. This might be because deeper ploughing drains the land better — I don't know.

Changes are not always harmful to wildlife. I wonder how much the population of birds like thrushes and blackbirds increased when the commons were enclosed and the hedges gave them increased nesting space and more fields were ploughed for them to feed upon.

Of course, farm buildings affect the appearance of the countryside as well. Originally, in this area, most of them were wooden, made with black, tarred boards. Generally, only the farmhouse and the stable were built of brick and, in every case, local brick, occasionally with pieces of flintwork as well. Almost every farm had a large, wooden barn, formerly used for threshing. A surprising number of these have been destroyed by fire within the last sixty years. I suppose by their very nature, they are liable to fire. Those now remaining either have been or are being converted into houses, because the urban population has become quite obsessed with preserving things of any age at all and these black-boarded barns are considered to be a feature of the countryside.

In the intervening period, with changes in farming, quite a lot of buildings have come and gone. During the 'twenties and 'thirties most farms had added to them a tin-roofed dutch barn with a curved roof and many of those are now rusting away. They were put up to protect the hay that was needed for the increased livestock kept in at that time, and now, with decreased livestock, they are more or less redundant unless they have been adapted for other purposes, like housing grain driers. Then, during the war and the post-war boom, tower silos of various sorts arrived on almost every farm, silos for preserving grass and, occasionally, for storing grain. A good many of these have already disappeared — an extraordinarily short life for this fashion of preserving grass. After them, during the next thirty years came the big concrete and asbestos wide-span buildings, for housing livestock and afterwards used for grain storage and the large, modern machinery. The development of these has almost stopped and quite a number are redundant, standing deserted in corners of fields, because they are no longer required and because asbestos is now considered dangerous.

Now, far fewer buildings are wanted for modern farming. Grain going away in bulk only requires a short storage period. It is stored in bins of one sort or another and does not require big sheds. Artificial fertilizers now come in weatherproof bags and some people do not even bother to put them in a building at all. Anyway, the larger farms require fewer sets of premises. Everywhere, farm buildings stand empty and derelict, even some that are quite new.

One additional disfigurement of the countryside, developing apace, is a product of urban prosperity and of middle-class commuting. More and more small pieces of land, formerly used for farming, have been taken over by horsey-culture and everywhere are groups of children's ponies and fields disfigured by ill-constructed jumps with, sometimes, a scruffy-looking shelter in a corner of the field, so that urban 'daddies' can provide their daughters with status symbols.

At what stage would you like to freeze all this?

GROVE FARM

My father seems to have been anxious to prove that his house had a history; as a matter of fact, it was a small farmhouse heavily modernized by him at the turn of the century. But the discovery of two or three 17th-century musket balls in one of the walls when alterations were being done, was enough to prove that there had been a skirmish in the Civil War, somewhere there outside, and one conjures up a picture of perhaps a few Royalists hiding in the house from the overwhelming Parliamentarian population of the area. As a matter of fact, that is unlikely to coincide with the facts. There is no record of any skirmish anywhere in the whole parish, and although the population of the area was strongly Parliamentarian, they kept their heads down and didn't get into trouble, either before, during, or after.

And then, there's the naming of the house. It was Little Grove Farm when my father bought it. And the discovery in about 1910 that the field opposite was called Briary Close, seemed to indicate a corruption of the word 'priory', so the house name was changed to Little Grove Priory. In fact, the word 'briary' was a corruption of the word 'barley' and there never had been any priory on or near the site, although I discovered as recently as the 1970s that there had been a house on the site in the Middle Ages long before the house my father converted. I don't think I ever believed my father's history of that house, but then I've never believed anything I was told by my parents, so there was nothing surprising about that.

When, in late 1918, my father bought the neighbouring Grove Farm, everything changed. There were genuine ruins in which we played, and around which all my life I have woven a history probably just as spurious as my father's history of his house. I used to sit, as a small boy, on the bank of the moat that goes round the farm, close my eyes and imagine that I was there when they were constructing it. I imagined I saw files of men and women carrying baskets of dirt from the bottom, up the ramps at the corner of the moat, dumping it in the heaps that are still there, and carrying back baskets of stones picked up from the inside of the moat, to make the walls. I had a job imagining how they would be dressed; in my mind they looked like

children's story-book illustrations of Robin Hood, only a bit scruffier from the work they were doing.

The building standing, surrounded by the moat, is marked on the map as 'chapel, remains of' which I think reinforced in my then widowed mother's mind the story about the priory. Actually, if it was ever used as a chapel at all, it would have been during the 18th century by some obscure non-conformist sect long after it had been abandoned as a farmhouse.

Then there were the walls around the edge of the moat, with the foundations of the two little towers where the entrance must have been. They were full up with rubbish, so we started to dig the rubbish out. We found some steps, which was most exciting, but they led nowhere except to a dirt floor. We started to clean out the other tower and we found at the bottom of that a very small well, filled with big stones; big dressed stones which had obviously been part of pillars and lintels, and we started laboriously to get these out. We got down maybe four or five feet, then disaster hit. Early one morning, some animals got out and a heifer, leaping across our gaping well-hole, slipped in and got stuck. The farmworkers all had to erect a scaffolding over her and lift her out with pulley blocks and we were forbidden to explore any further.

We were also told that we wouldn't find anything because 'old Peter', a farmworker, had found it all some thirty or forty years before. During one dinner break he had been seen looking around the moat walls and then he had gone off, never to come back to work again, so it was assumed he had found something that had enabled him to live without working again for the rest of his life. A highly improbable story, I think; more likely he had just had enough.

In later life I have been quite obsessed with who might have dug the moat and built the so-called chapel which I converted back into a house about twenty-five years ago and in which I still live. I have found very little: the original enclosure was dated early 12th century and there were two virgates of land (about sixty acres) — you still see the boundaries quite clearly — but two or three times it was re-possessed by the Crown for various undisclosed misdemeanours.

More recently I read about a 13th-century family who owned most of the parish of Chesham, called Sifrewast. They had a history of cattle stealing and illegal tree-felling, things of that sort. I was convinced that they must have lived in my house. They must have started to build themselves a small castle or fortress, certainly never finished; the wall around the edge of the moat only exists on three

sides, so that they would have been able to repel adversaries coming
from the east, north or south, but not from the west. Their
adversaries would have had to swim the moat first, but that would not
have been very difficult. As soon as I consulted any real expert, the
idea of any Sifrewast living in my house was dismissed, though they
certainly did own it for a while. I was disappointed, so I still don't
know who lived here.

Among the stories circulating locally about the place is one about a
hole that appeared under what is now my dining-room floor, around
the turn of the century, which the farm people were curious to
investigate. Squire Lowndes forbade them, probably because he
didn't want to have to pay them. But the farmworkers decided that he
had a more sinister motive, that the hole held some dark and dirty
secret.

By the time I was around, the story of the hole had so developed in
the thoughts of the people working on the farm that it had become in
their minds the entrance to a passage leading all the way to
Berkhamsted Castle. The construction of this would have been an
impossible feat in the Middle Ages — the building dates from 1128
— difficult enough these days even with modern tunnelling
equipment. There's a drop of some two hundred feet for a start and a
valley to cross, and why would anybody have gone to all that trouble
anyway?

In certain parts of north Germany every farmhouse has a stone,
inscribed with the name of the man who first built the farm, and the
date of building it. I wish we had that custom here. I would love to
know when every building on my farm had been built, together with
the name and details of the builder. Just a bit of human interest.
From time to time, through various county record books, I have
picked up a bit of information, but not really enough. I do know that
at the time of the Napoleonic wars the farmer here was a John
Barnes. He had the same number of horses as Benny Wingrove, the
tenant here in 1918, proving that the farm was the same size. I know
that in the mid 1600s it was occupied by a man called Bunn, so
presumably it was he who built the 17th-century barn, now converted
into a house. But who was it who decided to let the original house fall
into disrepair, and build a new one around about 1700? And why did
they do it when it wasn't nearly such a good house anyway? Of
course, the locals said it was because the old house was haunted and
the owners couldn't bear to live there.

I've always boasted about the age of my house, which led to my being heavily put down on one occasion. I was saying to a Charolais breeder from southern Alabama, Paul Wyndham, that I lived in a very old house, that building started over seven hundred years ago and was completed in 1565. He said, 'That's a pity. Never mind, the price you are selling your Charolais cattle, you will soon be able to pull it down and have a new one!'

I was a bit put down by that. But then, what does one expect from Americans? Didn't they half bulldoze the iron age camp in Whelpley Hill, half a mile from my house, which is much older than anything I have got? They bulldozed that half flat during the war, just to make room for a couple of bombers which could easily have been parked somewhere else.

DABBERFIELD

There is a field on Grove Farm called Dabberfield, which is like a map of four hundred years of history. It is called Dabberfield because a 'dabber' in the Chilterns is a pebble and the stones here are flat pebbles, not sharp flints as they are in all the surrounding fields. From here, with a little imagination, you can see every change that has taken place in agriculture, and in this bit of countryside, since the forests were first cleared.

Thinking of forests, in the distance, to the west, are Hockeridge Woods, bigger than most of the Chiltern woods; probably parts of them have always been woodland. When I was a very small boy, it seemed so big to me that I thought it was a forest and I remember when I first went away to school, arguing furiously with a boy from Hampshire that Hockeridge Woods were much bigger than the New Forest. I argued with such force that he almost believed me until, one day later, I took him there to show it to him and he laughed and the woods got smaller in my eyes.

The valley immediately in front of us is a pretty little valley, just ordinary green belt, of outstanding natural beauty. We have never had an energetic parish councillor to push for it to be designated as such, or else the planners have never visited it — certainly there are less attractive bits of country which are zoned as of outstanding natural beauty — but it is green belt and it will remain that way.

Arnold Baines says that if you are scheduling or describing a piece of country, you must start in the east and move around the way the sun goes. That is the way it was always done with ancient maps and lists of estates, so, I had better do the same thing.

This field was originally part of Sales Farm and Sales farmhouse is to the east of us — a little out of sight but I know it is there. The name comes from the man who owned it in 1600, Josiah Sale. I've no idea how long his family continued to own it but, in the end, the land was joined to Grove Farm to make one farm. The house itself was divided into a number of small workers' cottages so, at the end of the 19th century, there were at least five, or perhaps six families living there — almost a little hamlet. Then things changed, and in the Depression less labour was needed on the farms and, in any case, the cottages were very small and dilapidated. In the mid 'thirties, they were all condemned and the families moved out into council houses. Somebody came along and bought the wreck and turned it into a highly desirable residence for a commuter, and so it has remained: a story which could be repeated a thousand times all over southern Britain and hundreds of times in the Chilterns.

Moving round towards the south, the first thing you see are the trees that surround Grove Farm on the banks of the moat. Whoever dug those defences for himself organized, almost without doubt, the clearance of this particular area of the forest, leaving, a little farther round to the west, Deans Wood, which belonged to a family called Dean from the 15th to the late 17th century. They evidently worked the timber within the wood itself, which is riddled with sawpits, and managed somehow or other, I suppose, to make a living out of no more than six and a half acres of woodland.

At that point, one is reminded of the fact that the whole area is riddled with chalkpits, evidence of efforts to improve the land just here and perhaps farther away over many hundreds of years. There are so many chalkpits, surrounded by little groups of trees, that it is hard to believe that all the chalk was used in this immediate area; perhaps it was worked as an industry and sold to farmers a little bit farther away. You can see a road in the distance in the south-west. This is known as Two Dells Road and I am sure all the people living in the area, both the natives and the commuters, think that it has got something to do with two dells in the ground by the road or the two dips in the road. Nothing of the sort — it is because, surrounded by all these chalkpits, was once a farm and it was owned, again in Elizabethan times, by James and William Dell, two Dells. Dozens of their descendants are, no doubt, still around but I doubt if any of them knows about it.

Next there is a little group of modern houses in a triangular piece of land. This was not owned by any of the surrounding farmers; it was owned, when I first remember it, by the pub at Ashley Green nearly a mile away and was alleged to have originally been the pound in which the parish shut straying cattle until they were bailed out by their owners. Then, in the 'thirties, some enterprising person built houses on it as it was not much good for farming anyway, this tiny triangle.

On the horizon, between these cottages and the outline of Hockeridge Woods, is the village of Ashley Green. It has been there a long time but most of its buildings are modern. Its church and its school date from the mid 19th century and were the work of a family who we shall come across in a few minutes, the Smith Dorriens, who were evidently very benevolent landowners in the area. All the time, we have been looking across the valley, but if you look down into it you see a number of different things. You can see folds in the ground, which represent the old field boundaries which have been done away with — folds created by ploughing down the hill one way and throwing the soil all in one direction so it piled up on one side of the hedge, and when the hedge was removed the bank remained.

By the way, the valley itself has a name, not at all a romantic one. It is marked on the map as Bournegutter — 'bourne' referring to the fact that, every few years, a fair-sized river springs up in it and flows down in the direction of Hertfordshire. But 'gutter' — surely they could have thought of something better when they made the first Ordnance Survey maps? But they used the valley as a boundary between Buckinghamshire and Hertfordshire in the very early days, and since that part of Herts is known as Dacorum which means 'Danish', it has been said that this was the boundary between Denmark and England in the year 900 A.D. Perhaps somebody dug a ditch as a county boundary and, because it filled with water, they called that the Bournegutter and not the valley itself.

In the middle of the field, just below my feet, there is a clump of bushes. This is not a chalkpit, but a well — a mile from the nearest house. There does not seem to be much point in having it there, but of course it was very near where the river springs up every few years. I think that perhaps once upon a time there was a very serious drought and the people in Ashley Green or Whelpley Hill, or maybe at Sales Farm or Grove Farm, thought that they would dig a well where they knew they would find water. I imagine them frantically digging; wells could be dug surprisingly quickly by experienced well-diggers. This one is about forty feet deep and has always got water in the bottom. It is lined with bricks at the top and flints lower down, so it is probably pretty old. According to a local story, some time in the last century a man in Bovingdon, about two and a half miles away, called Harry King, stole a hindquarter of beef — some people say a whole side of beef — carried it to the well and suspended it on a rope inside (where he thought nobody would find it and it would be kept cool), intending to come at nights and cut off pieces to sell or use until it had all gone. One old local man, Walt Batchelor, told me he remembered having to back a waggon over the well to lower a rope down to haul the stolen meat out again. If Harry King had really carried even a quarter of beef all that way, I hope he was not punished too severely for it because it must have demanded a tremendous effort.

Just on top of the hill beyond the well is a farm called Harriots End Farm. I have often wondered who Harriot was, and what her end was. Behind that you can just see what was obviously in the past a park — big trees round the boundary and big trees out in the field. That belonged to Haresfoot House where the benevolent Smith Dorriens, who built the church and school at Ashley Green, lived; they also organized a trainload of London navvies to pull down the fences that Lord Brownlow had erected on Berkhamsted Common and so prevented its enclosure in the 1850s.

An ancestor of that family called Colonel Dorrien, living in the same spot, was mentioned in Arthur Young's survey of agriculture in Hertfordshire in the late 18th century. Colonel Dorrien had, it seems, a very good method of using chalk, whereby he had it dug from his pits and put into the cattle yards; the cattle were littered up with straw all winter and lay warm and dry on the straw and chalk, and both the manure and chalk were carted out together the following spring to fertilize the Colonel's land.

His actual farm was not Harriots End Farm, it was another one which you can see through the trees in the winter time, but not so well now in the summer. It is quite a big place which, together with Harriots End, is well farmed by an energetic Scottish family with large herds of cattle; they are tenants of an insurance firm as so many farmers are now.

Round further, the valley winds down towards the road between Berkhamsted and Hemel Hempstead. There is no evidence anywhere of the Green Belt being encroached upon. You cannot see the new town of Hemel Hempstead in the summer, although you just might in the winter. The only invasion of it since the war are two hefty lines of pylons taking electricity from Hemel Hempstead to Chesham and on to Amersham.

North-east and very close to us, only a hundred yards away, is what appears to be a long, narrow spinney on the side of the hill. In fact, it is a vastly overgrown hedge where, because the hill was originally steep, the ploughing of ground away from the hedge one side, and towards it on the other (which means you can never get really close because of having to turn) has vastly extended the scope of the hedge itself so that it is twenty yards or more wide and the shrubs and the trees from the hedge have encroached on the land on both sides. This is what is known locally as a 'hedgebrew' or 'brow' and it is a favourite place for badgers. In the spring it is absolutely full of white violets.

We have now gone round 360° and, of course, I have missed things. First of all, we are standing right on the edge of a chalkpit which, like all the others, has become a small wood. This was one where the chalk was carted, with the horse and cart, out of the side of the hill, whereas so many of the others that one can see, little ones dotted about, were mined and the chalk pulled out with a windlass. This one, dug out sideways, is shallow and quite wide so that the horses and carts could be used.

The other thing I missed is the little belt of fir trees which I myself planted on the south-east boundary of Dabberfield. I planted it on a raised strip about six yards wide which represented, originally, a permanent headland, a system quite common in this area and mentioned by Cobbett whereby a piece was left round all the fields to turn the machinery on to save damaging the crop. This piece was kept in grass and was mown to make hay but, of course, the custom died out in the mid 19th century when hay ceased to be mowed by hand because you could not do these little strips with machinery. All the other permanent headlands have been done away with and ploughed up. I preserved just this one by planting the trees on it and nobody else but me will ever recognize what it represented: a system long since out of use.

All around you is evidence of modern science: tractor-wheel marks in the corn, known as tramlines, where the sprays and fertilizers have been used; variations in the crop caused by mal-distribution of the fertilizer; modern crop varieties, and heavy yields in prospect.

Some of the field names are ancient ones and relate to former owners: Two Dells, Wethereds and Sales. Others are functional ones, which we may be able to date back just as far: Dabberfield, Stoneylands, Hangings, Broadbulk, Nineacres (this one a joke because it never was). Superimposed upon all this is the modern pattern of much larger fields, large and probably nameless enclosures. The hedges between them are infinitely varied where the ancient hedges remain, and uniform and regular where modern hedges have been planted within the last hundred years or so.

But it is the little woods and the big woods, that really form the scenery, and all of them came into existence because somebody dug a hole in the ground that could not be ploughed, so it had to be planted, and if it was not planted it grew up on its own into a spinney or a wood.

ALL THE WOODEN SPOONS
OF ENGLAND

Go back to about 1930, into Chesham High Street, and all the side streets leading off it were pretty empty of traffic. Be there around about knocking-off time in the factories, and from every one you would see men coming, pushing little trucks on wheels, or carrying bags, full of broken wooden spades and spoons and pieces of wooden hoops. Taking home to burn on their fires that part of their work which had failed, because in those days most of Chesham lived from working in beechwood. If you had talked to one of the men he would have said that all the wooden spoons of England were made in Chesham, and most of the wooden spades as well. So many millions of wooden spoons came out of Chesham in the 'twenties and 'thirties, so many countless millions of wooden spades for children to play with on the beach. Children's wooden hoops, too, made of beech, you saw them stacked up by the score outside the factories.

The whole town was very, very expert in dealing with beechwood. They knew exactly which logs to use for which purpose, how dry they had to be before you turned them, and how they needed to be handled afterwards to stop them splitting. And still they had enough damaged ones to take to their wives to keep the fire burning at home.

What they made ranged from the mass-produced ordinary wooden spoons and spades of Howard Bros, Jesse Wrights and several other smaller works, to the really high-quality stuff, the sort of wooden kitchenware that was sold in Aspreys and such shops in London. I remember when the first Queen Mary was launched, seeing the most magnificent, huge salad bowls, maybe two foot across and made out of a single piece of wood: some in beech and some in sycamore, which was white, made, I understood, by Ted Arnold, who worked as a skilled woodturner for Jesse Wrights.

Elsewhere in the town they made things like very cheap toy cricket bats, butter pats, and yokes for carrying buckets. And my old friend Bill Moulder and others made barn shovels for James East & Sons — huge, wide, wooden shovels made of a single piece of beech that had to be cut just right across the grain so that it didn't split; these could be used for moving grain on farms, shovelling malt in breweries, work of that sort where a large, light shovel was required. Bill Moulder could have described his craft in the most exact terms. He was a man who lacked formal education but who was one of the wisest men I have ever known, and with a marvellous Chesham accent which he used to put himself across so well. I looked upon it as an awful missed chance, it could have been the woodturner's story. Of course there were many others like him, but he was the one I knew best. Few wise men become craftsmen anymore. They are all educated now, and I suppose they are much better off, and the nation is better off by having the use of their wisdom.

It's a funny thing that the whole nation knows what our larger neighbour, High Wycombe, has always done: it has made furniture, Windsor chairs and things like that. Whereas our industry has disappeared, theirs has carried on and become modernized.

It started in the beech woods with people called 'bodgers' making parts of the chairs, right in the beech wood where the beech was grown; they were finished in factories. The bodgers lived there too and the Buckinghamshire word has become part of the English language (the new meaning deriving from the fact that bodgers half finished their work). Letting the wood mature to the right point, they cut the tree up over a sawpit and turned it, using a treadle machine in a hut on the spot; then they sold it on to the chair factories to be finished. Chairmaking developed into a large industry in High Wycombe. Those craftsmen are no more and now there is mass production of G-Plan, Ercol, and so on. Like the industry of Chesham, that of High Wycombe was founded on the beech, though other woods were used as well; nowadays it is all imported materials and plywood.

Nobody has sung the praises of Chesham the way they should have done, the skill of its woodturners and the variety of its products. It has been mentioned and shown in exhibitions, but nobody ever appreciates the full quality of what the town used to make. What is left is but a pale shadow. Maybe one or two little workshops making a few wooden bowls from elm and other woods. No more huge bowls for the Queen Mary. If anybody wants big bowls they are imported from other countries.

I don't know when this wooden ware industry in Chesham started. Certainly the local landowners started planting the beech for their own use and to sell to High Wycombe early in the 17th century; this must have been the boom time for planting, to judge by the look of the trees in the woods and such history as one can glean. Beech was by far the easiest wood to turn, and very suitable for charcoal burning if you didn't want it for turning. Beech dominated everything. Not naturally, but artificially because it was the crop that the landowners wanted. Like the brewers wanted barley and the millers wanted wheat, the woodturners wanted beech.

The primeval forests of oak and thorn had long since gone for the most part, although there may have been little scraps remaining. Every odd bit of land, every bit of land too steep or too poor to cultivate, every small piece ruined for cultivation by the digging of clay, stones or chalk was planted with beech trees and only beech trees. And apart from the few oaks around the outside of the woods which, I suppose, they thought would always be wanted, for building, for gateposts and fencing and so on, everything else was taken out. To produce a wood of nothing but beech is quite a sophisticated business. Beech is delicate when it is young and has to be protected. So in the latter years of the beech planting the custom grew up of planting larch, or sometimes Scots pine, with it. This grew up much faster than the beech, protected it from the frost, and drew it up tall with no low branches so there wouldn't be any knots in the wood. Then, at twenty or thirty years the larch and fir were removed. I have no idea when this practice started, or who brought it in; somebody must know.

And so, after two hundred years of this activity, nearly all the woods in our part of the Chilterns were beech with just these few oaks around the outside. Elm trees, a few ash trees, and oak trees in the hedges, but the woods just beech. Beech in a hedge isn't any good, it grows too knotty; elm doesn't like growing in woods, and who wants a lot of elm anyway, just enough for coffins, no more.

During the last sixty years, big changes have taken place. During the 'twenties, farmers who were hard up and who owned their freeholds sold their hedgerow trees for whatever they could get. This started a fundamental change in the countryside of which so many people complain. It reduced the oaks and elms. Those who owned small beech woods felled them as well and could rarely afford to replant. And where they did this, mixed woods sprang up. Cherry galore, because cherry does well in the Chilterns and cherry seeds sew well as the birds spread them everywhere. Cherry, however, has a limited life, forty or fifty years, and is already in many cases beginning to die.

To take a look at woodland in the two parishes, Ashley Green and Latimer, starting near the town of Chesham: high above Chesham Vale there is Francis Wood, a wood which has been protected because it is so near the town. I don't know when it was planted — not so very long ago I suspect because the trees aren't very big — but it has been left unthinned, unfelled, for a long time and as a result the trees are dying. They are not dying of any disease, they are not even, as with so many others, dying of old age; they are dying for lack of water because there is not enough water on the poor, chalky land to support a big population of trees. If they had been thinned as they should have been, they would still be vigorous and dark green in the summer instead of pale yellow.

Move round to Ashley Green and you come to Hockeridge Woods, covering the boundary between Buckinghamshire and Hertfordshire, and much bigger than any other woods in the area. Because it is mentioned in early documents, I suspect it includes a fragment of primeval wood which has been maintained, constantly renewed and replanted — managed, on the whole, over the years by benevolent landowners. The effect is of patches of different species, reflecting the fashions of the time each was planted. There are patches of mixed wood which is perhaps the original; patches of beech; and patches of fir planted in the early 'twenties when that was the fashion of the day; patches that were felled during the war and have since grown up of their own accord, full of sycamore and ash from which the seeds blow everywhere, other patches replanted with a mixture of fir and beech. A great variety, but all fairly orderly and in plantations.

And then you come round to my farm where there are several small woods. There is Deans Wood, only six and a half acres, which belonged in the 16th and 17th centuries to a family called Dean. It has a number of sawpits, and I visualize this family Dean making a living out of it, cutting up timber within their own wood, dragging it over the sawpits, and some poor lad lying in the bottom with the sawdust falling in his face while Mr Dean stood on the top, pulling the saw upwards. That wood too is a mixture of trees, a sort of small-scale Hockeridge, a victim of the fashions which have influenced me. First, in my desire to preserve a pure beech wood, I planted nothing but beech; later, I added groups of larch; and, last of all, when I became aware of their existence, I planted beech imported from South America, to introduce variety and because it is alleged that squirrels won't touch them.

Next to Deans Wood, round my farm to the east, is a wood known as The Banks. This wood is on the banks of the moat which never would have grown trees naturally. It was planted by the Lowndes family, I suspect in about the late 18th century, since all the beech has recently become mature, some sold and replaced by myself. I counted the rings from a sawn tree two years ago and there were over two hundred of them.

Further to the east on the boundary of the county are two woods that are quite typical of what happened when woods fell into the hands of timber merchants in the 'thirties: Great Wood, a long, narrow wood near the county boundary with Herts on a ridge of poor land, and Bush Wood. Both were victims of a timber merchant who cut everything saleable out of them and then simply abandoned them. Great Wood is now a wood again, but mixed, all sorts of species; again cherry, ash and sycamore predominating, and the beech in a minority. Bush Wood suffered a particular fate: the bulk of it was used by the Americans as a bomb dump during the war so nothing much was left and I ploughed it up, preserving just a little bit, only about two or three acres of what had originally been sixteen.

Then, around quite a distance to the south, is Cowcroft Wood: over forty acres of the most interesting wood, I believe, in the whole of the area. Interesting because it is what nature does, left to itself. It is not cut down and abandoned, it has grown out of abandoned industrial workings and old brickworks from the 16th century onwards. Workers merely dug the clay to make the bricks, left a hole and moved on somewhere else, and every possible species of tree has moved in. The result is that there are very many — over thirty — species there, and a great variety of wildlife, attracted by the different species of plants and trees.

Finally, to the south of Latimer parish, is the Latimer estate — a typical 18th-century, well laid out, landowners' estate, where Lord Chesham used to live. There are orderly woods of beech and fir, orderly avenues of lime, and parkland, groves of spruce — everything spaced out in the best possible way for sporting purposes so that the hounds could draw for fox-hunting and the beaters could beat for the well-placed guests at the House to shoot. There was beech grown for sale, ash to repair his Lordship's vehicles, and oak to repair his buildings, and a few elm to sell for locals to be buried in.

Alas, at the beginning of the last war, some of the best woods had to be taken for the war effort. It was found that beech was suitable for plywood out of which Mosquito planes could be made at Hatfield: a processing plant was set up to use the beech from Latimer, which was of good quality, and the main woods were all flattened and removed in their entirety — all pure beech of the highest quality. After the war, with the woods taken over by the Forestry Commission, the normal, orderly mixture of conifers and beech was planted which, I suppose, in the end will be thinned so that only the beech remains — I hope so although I'll never see it.

In that one estate at Latimer, you see that timber is a crop, planted, grown and managed by man for his use like any other crop. Altered by neglect, sometimes beautified by neglect, but in the end a crop.

Chesham's beautiful wooden ware has all gone and the free broken bits of firewood for the woodturners to take home have gone as well. The new generation of woodlands, when they mature, will probably be turned into pulp — cardboard, hardboard, blockboard, chipboard, plywood, some boring industrial product nobody can associate with any tree at all. And there is no real interest in where it came from. Nobody, but nobody, will remember the woodturners of Chesham and the beautiful things they made; not even the millions of children who have played on the beach with their wooden spades.

FRIENDS OF THE TREES
the great storm of 1987

The early morning of October 16th, 1987 was when I got punished for my lifelong love and obsession with trees. I woke up to find no electricity, and no telephone to complain about the electricity. I tried to get out to my car to go to another phone to complain, but I couldn't get out of my house for the trees which had fallen in all directions.

The whole of southern England was punished for its obsession with trees. The commuters from the northern Home Counties who complain every time anybody lops, tops or cuts a tree anywhere within the county of Buckinghamshire, or its neighbours, couldn't get to work because of the trees which had fallen down on the railway line and the trees which had fallen on the roads. And about half of them couldn't get any breakfast because, like me, their electricity had been cut off. Bit of a joke, really, considering the efforts people make to preserve trees, when the trees came back at them in this hostile manner, just because there was a little wind. I didn't see the joke at half past five in the morning.

The English seem to get terribly emotional and irrational about trees. Hardly a week goes by without an incident somewhere. Once our local paper told of an elderly gentleman who sat in front of a bulldozer and successfully protected a tree. A few years ago, I remember reading that a tree surgeon had been killed trying to save a tree on a village green, which had been the subject of a great campaign to preserve it after other people thought it was dangerous. I wonder whether the campaigners felt guilty about that man's death.

The most remarkable case of tree irrationality was described to me a year or two ago by a Forestry Commission official. An extremely dedicated man, he really lived for his job, personally supervising several areas of woodland in the Chilterns. The previous day he had gone to one of his favourite plantations to see how it was doing. It was a thriving young plantation of mixed beech and larch, seven or eight years old and just beginning to look really good. He saw a minibus parked and — to his horror — a party of schoolchildren beating at the large trees with sticks and cutting them with penknives. He shouted loudly at them to desist and asked them what they were doing. They said they were on a nature walk with their schoolmistress and that: 'She told us to do this.'

He could hardly believe his ears. Sure enough though, after a few minutes, the schoolmistress turned up and said, 'How dare you stop my children doing what they were doing? I am teaching them about the environment.'

He said, 'Well, why are you encouraging them to cut the larch trees?'

She replied, 'Because they should not be planted here — they are foreigners and have no place on the Chilterns which is the proper place for beech trees.'

He told her in no uncertain terms that she had better take her class away, otherwise he would call the police to deal with them. Larch is, of course, a foreign tree; but so what, so are a lot of trees. Nobody would get as emotional as this about other plants. I have never heard of anybody attacking a field of potatoes on the grounds that they are an import from South America.

But we all think we know what should be planted in each particular area and are shocked at what other people do. Years ago the late Nye Bevan was a near neighbour of mine and I remember him denouncing the Forestry Commission, with considerable oratory, for planting pine forests in his native Wales instead of oaks. He referred to them somewhat theatrically as a forest of death — 'not only did they look gloomy but nothing grew under them. Bluebells and primroses had grown under the scrubby oaks when I was young but nothing grew under pines.' That is what everyone is saying now.

Before 1914 my father, according to the fashion of the day, planted Corsican pines, cypresses and sequoia from America. I never liked them so I didn't protect them from my cattle and a lot of them were destroyed. When I began planting, I started on ash which is a local species. Some of those I planted when I was very young still exist and have not, even now, reached maturity. I was for ash but against sequoia.

Later, when I was studying at university in the early 'thirties a dedicated lecturer indoctrinated us with the necessity of planting poplars in the hedgerows. He did not tell us that poplars need an enormous amount of moisture and would drain the sides of our fields almost dry unless they were extremely wet. He said they would grow very quickly and — almost with the light of battle in his eyes — that if we grew enough of them we would defeat the villainous Swedes who had a monopoly in matches because they grew aspens, out of which matchsticks were made. I took home from university some cuttings of various poplars. Duly, in less than forty years, they were fully mature. In the meantime they impoverished the edge of the field on which they were planted. Shallow roots were everywhere, getting in the way of cultivations. I thought it was time to sell them, at a high price, for making matchsticks. Alas, Bryant & May were no longer interested.

Just lately, I have been planting South American beech because experts assure me that the grey squirrel will ruin all the native European beech but will not touch the Chilean beech. In addition the Chilean beech grows very fast. This seems to be true; they are shooting up. I am not sure I accept the reason why squirrels do not attack them. It is said to be because the bark peels round and round instead of up and down like an ordinary beech, and that squirrels cannot work out how to hold on to the side of the tree and peel the bark off round and round. Somewhere in Britain a group of squirrels are probably sitting round considering the problem and working out how they can attack the Chilean beech, just as they do the native beech, when they start running out of suitable food. After all, the grey squirrel is an American and we all know how good the Americans are at working on new processes.

Everywhere in Britain, now there are self-appointed Friends of the Trees, who aim to preserve trees at all costs. This has some slightly comical results. I know of at least one developer of a site who had an order on him to preserve trees which did not exist. As a result he had to rush to a nurseryman to plant trees so that the order would have some validity. Not a bad end result but rather a silly way to achieve it.

A lot of these friends may well, in the end, prove to be enemies of trees. If you drive from Aylesbury in Buckinghamshire towards Tring, you could see over to your right — to the south of the road — the whole Chiltern escarpment clad with beech woods which were nearly all dying, probably because they were too old. If they had been exploited commercially some years ago and cut out when they reached their optimum size for timber, they would by now have been replaced by natural regeneration, if not by re-planting. The preservation of trees beyond their natural life can be dangerous not only to people, but also to the trees themselves, as any hurricane will prove.

But governments and the Forestry Commission are followers of fashion too. Ten years ago we were told to mix larch with the beech we were planting, even if we wanted to have a beech wood, so that the larch would protect the young beech and be removed after a year or two. Now we are forbidden to plant larch or any other firs. So the schoolmistress has won. Until the fashion changes.

But who am I to talk about people being irrational? For the past year, at the age of seventy-four, I have been planting oak trees. They cannot be mature in my life; they cannot be mature in my sons' lives; they cannot be mature in my grandchildren's lives. How daft can you get?

SINGING AND WHISTLING

Nobody sings or whistles anymore. People always used to sing or whistle when they were at work; a number of the elderly people we interviewed for *Seventy Summers* remarked that you could always hear men whistling in the fields, or singing. In those days, too, when many things were delivered to the door, when there was a butcher's boy and a grocer's boy as well as just a paper boy, the butcher's boy was always whistling when he came. Women sang when they were doing their housework, either hymns if they were that way inclined, or popular songs of the time. Of course, one can remember clearly the songs of the first world war, but also all sorts of popular songs immediately afterwards. The girls who worked in my mother's house sang 'Swanee' and 'I'm forever blowing bubbles', and things of that sort — but always they sung.

I could never whistle but I sang almost all the time when I was working by myself on the farm, and also when I was delivering milk in the early morning. I wasn't fussy about what I sang. Though I've never been a churchgoer, hymn tunes come easy, so I sang them, but also the popular songs of the time. We still have a young person who delivers the papers to our door at seven o'clock each morning. I don't know the sex of the deliverer, but I would if they whistled or sang. I wonder if the entire British race has lost the power to whistle?

On farms, singing and whistling have partly gone out because the machines make so much noise you wouldn't be able to hear yourself. In fact on some of them you've got to wear earmuffs anyway to stop yourself going deaf. Though that didn't really stop me: I've met several people recently whose first memory of coming to see me on my farm was of me driving an old Fordson tractor and singing above the sound of the engine. I did have a powerful voice.

Listeners are not missing very much by not hearing the singing or whistling, because I don't suppose any of us were much in tune, but we ourselves are missing something very satisfying. I am sure it does you good to bellow out your favourite song at the top of your voice. Why has everyone stopped doing it?

I suppose the walkmans have something to do with it. Perhaps the young person who delivers our papers in the morning has got her or his stereo on, so we hear absolutely nothing until the papers flop through the letterbox onto the floor. And perhaps women don't sing at their housework because they, too, are operating machines, or because so many of them have the radio on all the time. There are people I know who cannot be in a room on their own without the radio; I am sure they'd find it much more relaxing singing to themselves.

I think perhaps that people are also more inhibited than they used to be and would be afraid to sing in front of other people. It didn't seem to bother us before. I remember going on a building site around about 1950 — and I think this is the very last time I heard anybody singing, really singing, on a building site — and a marvellous rendering of 'Ave Maria' was coming over the air, sung by a really beautiful tenor voice. I asked the foreman who it was, and he said, 'Oh that's Bernard Puddephatt, he's always had a good voice.' I don't know what's happened to him, but I haven't heard any tenors on building sites lately, and I rather think if anybody started up they would be shouted down because they were interfering with the enjoyment of the radios that are hung on scaffolds all over the place, playing forth their stuff and interspersed with idiotic comments from disc jockeys.

But then I am the same as all the others. For the last five years I haven't sung any more. Perhaps it's just that I'm losing my voice. Before that, Florence and I, if we were going anywhere by car, used to sing together almost all the time and it helped to make the journey pass most pleasantly (more for me than her, because she had the better voice). However, the next damp day I shall go out in the wood and attempt to sing, at the top of my voice, 'So deep is the night', followed by an odd hymn or two, then 'Early one morning'. I'll choose a damp day because I always seem to sing better when it is damp; in fact at one stage the family said if I was singing it meant it was going to rain shortly!

I USED TO SING

I used to sing,
Not prettily, but very loud.
I used to swim,
Not fast, but long.
I never dived or jumped.
I rarely ran, and very slow,
But walked as well as any man.
But now just hobble
Sit and lie.
My voice a croak.
My head's alright, I think.

T.H.

Tin Racketing
and All That

The attitude of the rural population of Buckinghamshire in, say, 1920, towards sex, marriage and morals was not what one might probably imagine. Even in Victorian times it was much more tolerant than people might think. Our impressions about what people thought about such matters in previous generations are secondhand, given to us primarily by people who wrote books or in newspapers at the time. And they were overwhelmingly middle-class people: middle classes with a rigid idea about sex within marriage and blanket disapproval of sex outside marriage and who over-protected their daughters but not, of course, their sons.

The general population, living and working on farms and in the small towns, wanted their daughters to make good marriages; they didn't want them to get into trouble and have illegitimate children, but if they did, were in the end pretty tolerant and accepting. I have a mental picture of young people in the past who never met the boy or girl next door except by arrangement at some social event. It was a bit different if you were working together in the fields. You worked together in the fresh air and sunshine, sat down by the hedge to have your lunch and were close to nature, and nature was sure to assert itself quite quickly. Provided people lived up to their responsibilities, nobody really minded in the long term, despite the social conventions of the day.

It is significant that the squire of Chesham in Victorian and Edwardian times, Squire Billy Lowndes, had a number of illegitimate children. He both publicly acknowledged and provided for them, and if you look in the county archives relating to the Lowndes estate in Chesham, it's all recorded there. As a child I knew all about it, everybody in Chesham knew all about it, and they didn't appear to think any ill, either of Billy Lowndes, about whom they joked tolerantly, or about the resultant illegitimate families, some of whom got on very well in life. But he was approved of because he provided for them properly.

In the countryside, and in small industrial towns among the working population, there was always a high illegitimacy rate. People talked about it and gossiped about it when it first happened, and then

they shut up and let people get on with their lives and many, many couples lived together successfully and faithfully without ever bothering to get married. Sometimes the family relationships were quite complicated. I knew one family, brought up in the same house, all with different surnames: same mother, different fathers; they opted for whichever surname they liked. People joked about it, but nobody thought any ill of them.

Of course it was different among the very religious, chapel-going population, the extra-respectable working class and trades people. They, if they broke conventions and rules, probably got themselves thrown out of their chapel, although I believe repentance was almost always accepted in the end. Perhaps they joined another chapel: there was a choice of eight or nine in Chesham alone in those days.

I remember a case where an elder of a local chapel was found in a compromising situation in-between the pews with the chapel cleaner. The scandal flew around the town like mad with the result that he had to leave the chapel and she had to get another job as a cleaner, but, as far as I am aware, they both lived happily ever after. Nobody ostracized them. Nobody scrawled 'whore' on her wall, just as nobody had scrawled rude graffiti on Billy Lowndes's wall. Both men had lived up to their responsibilities. It was a proper morality, in that anybody, married or unmarried, who didn't look after his family properly was ostracized and frowned upon.

Occasionally, a village collectively — or a street, or the workers in a factory — would feel that one of their members was going wrong, developing a friendship with a second woman which would result in trouble for his family, and their way of dealing with it was to take direct action to discourage him. This is where the tin-racketing came in, not I believe very often, but it existed as a threat.

My mother-in-law, who knew just about everything that took place in Chesham, once pointed an old man out to me, and told me that when he was young his mates at the factory knew he was starting something with another woman. They thought it ought to be stopped: he wasn't earning enough to keep two families. Their morality was a practical one, combined with a certain sympathy in a world that was hard on women. The other woman lived at the end of the town and, one night, when the man came out of her house there, in the then unlit streets of Chesham, in every dark corner and behind the walls and round the corners were his workmates, beating tins and buckets and making loud noises, and they followed him all the way home. 'That taught him a lesson', my mother-in-law said, with a sly smile. I think she rather approved of it. Anyway, she said he then remained happily married for the rest of his life. I wonder whether there was a moral for me in the tale.

More dramatic was the story of a magistrate from a local village. He had a lady friend at the other side of the common and the villagers thought he was setting a bad example as a magistrate. One night when he came out of her house he was shocked to hear the sound of somebody beating a tin behind every hedge and bush all the way home. His wife, of course, must have heard it as well. I know he remained a magistrate; he certainly wouldn't have complained to the police. Perhaps he was more careful after that.

The practice of tin-racketing may well have gone on in other places; though the only other time I ever heard of anything similar was on holiday in Guernsey, many years ago.

In small communities, people tend to deal with their own problems. The minute book of the Chesham Baptists from 1712, still in existence, is a most revealing document. Eighteenth-century England must have been a pretty tolerant place; apparently the establishment and the magistracy allowed this little community of Baptists to deal with their own members, even in quite serious matters. Quarrels between neighbours didn't get heard in court, they were dealt with by the elders of the chapel who reasoned with the parties and then made them shake hands.

There was the case of one of the elders of the chapel who had cheated the local vicar — who was, after all, on the other side of the religious divide — over the tithe (one tenth of the harvest handed over to the Church) and was hauled in front of the elders and suitably punished. More extraordinary was the case of a member of the chapel who was held up for interfering with a thirteen-year-old girl. She, in quaint 18th-century English, gave her evidence:

'I was standing in the porch of brother Hawk's house when he offered me a biscuit and I said, [this seems rather to have been jumping to conclusions]: "I'll not be made a whore just for a biscuit." So he gave me two.'

Now, if there was a case at all, it was one that would nowadays be dealt with by the crown court. I suppose a tradition built up that where possible you dealt with your own problems. One of the disadvantages of that system was that the Baptists were dreadfully narrow-minded and persecuted their own members if they married out of their particular Church.

People were more tolerant in all sorts of ways and I believe that in the countryside they always have been, in relation to things like homosexuality, for example. In a town, I suppose, unthinking people looked upon every homosexual as a threat to their male children or something, I don't know, but they tended to get a rough time. In the countryside, living in an isolated situation, perhaps with his mother or with another old man, a homosexual was referred to as a 'Willjill'. There was tolerant interest, perhaps amazement, about the sides of life it was thought he was missing, but never any persecution so long as he lived in peace and didn't bother anybody else, which anticipated modern legislation by very many years. Altogether there has been a false impression of how things were sixty or seventy years ago.

I remember the countryside as being a relatively free and tolerant place, where local problems were dealt with and then quickly forgotten and nobody's life was permanently prejudiced and ruined by making just one or two mistakes. Maybe intolerance is spread by a close urban environment where people are forced into too close a proximity to one another. My belief is that fresh air and sunshine and sex in the fields breeds tolerance anyway.

CRIME IN THE COUNTRY

I suppose most of the population of Britain, who are mainly townsmen, imagine that country people are much more honest than townfolk. I don't think this has ever been a fact. While large-scale modern urban crime, like mugging, has never been a feature of the countryside, I've always thought that petty basic dishonesty, small-scale willingness to deprive other people of their property, was much more prevalent in rural areas.

I think the reason for this is fairly plain. If you are working for a farmer and growing crops like turnips or potatoes, you do not think much of helping yourself to a few, especially as some farmers would allow you to and some wouldn't. I think this breeds in the whole population of the countryside — even those who don't work in farms — the idea that crops are more or less there for the taking, as long as you can get away with it. Certainly, during the 'twenties and 'thirties when I was young, everybody took an extremely relaxed attitude towards helping themselves to our neighbour, Mr Mash's, crops. They didn't think of themselves as stealing. Mr Mash would think of them as thieves and would give them a hell of a telling-off if he caught them, but he would probably not prosecute them.

Poaching is another activity that adds to a casual attitude to people's possessions in the countryside. The court records in the 19th century show that it was a very common offence. But, while the magistrate looked upon it as a form of theft of another man's property, I do not think the general population did. They looked upon the game as something that was there, was wild, maybe protected by keepers but not put there by them; and therefore they had a perfect right to help themselves. This they continued to do, notwithstanding the fact that, until the end of the 19th century, the punishments for poaching were extremely severe.

The English Gamekeeper reports, in the middle of the last century, people being deported from Chesham for poaching. One of them was a man called Widdy Dell. When the book was republished recently, and I did a short foreword to it, Widdy's grand-daughter wrote to me and said she was happy to see her grandfather mentioned because she had heard all about his deportation to Australia, and she told me that he had come back, quite prosperous, some years later. Even in the 1920s when deportation had long finished, fines for poaching were very heavy and imprisonment was not uncommon. It did not stop the poaching; in fact I would have said poaching was at its most widespread at that time, because there was a high level of unemployment in Chesham and other small industrial towns and a little game or some rabbit was a very welcome addition to people's diets.

In a year like 1926, the year of the General Strike, you would find that a very high proportion of industrial workers in towns like Chesham had ferrets at the bottom of their gardens. They had no property on which to use the ferrets legally; they were kept entirely for poaching. Many of them had long nets as well because, in twos and threes, they had sufficient confidence to go out in the night, place nets around the rabbit warrens, send their ferrets in, and quietly net the rabbits. Legally, catching rabbits was not described as poaching but as trespassing 'in the pursuit of conies'.

Most poaching was done quietly with ferrets, dogs and nets, but sometimes it was done on a larger scale using guns, with the aim of getting the better of the keepers who were then employed almost everywhere to protect the game. I remember a classic case involving a Chesham man. Fred had been a successful, highly organized poacher for many years. He went out with others, taking guns if necessary, and made rapid raids on Lord Chesham's pheasants in Latimer. This shoot was his favourite, although he used others. It was all based on a quick raid, keeping the gamekeepers guessing and probably only going to each estate once or twice during the year. He knew every shoot's exact movements.

Fred had many sentences for poaching, first fines and then prison. Then, in the early 'thirties, he considered that he was getting a bit old for the job. He wrote a letter to Lord Chesham, which I have seen, starting very politely and very formally: 'My Lord, as you will know, I have a very long experience of poaching; indeed I know every inch of your estate. I also know every trick which a poacher could use, and now I am getting older, I am tired of occasionally going to prison, and I wish to apply for a job as a gamekeeper with you. I am sure I can most effectively do this work.' This, I suppose, is the classic case of a poacher trying to turn gamekeeper. He did not get the job. It would have demoralized the other gamekeepers who had been hunting Fred, with limited success, for a great many years.

Fred didn't look upon himself as a criminal. In his father's time he would have faced deportation and probably made a huge success for himself in Australia. Rather like a man called Chapman who, in the mid 19th century, lived in Grove Lane near to where I now live, and who wished to be deported. The worst rigours of Botany Bay being over, the later days of deportation were a form of assisted passage for immigration, if you were a misfit in this country. This man Chapman was not getting on very well. He had not got a very good job, so he stole something from a kitchen at Torrington Farm. He took it a distance away, hid it, and made sure he was seen; and he was duly arrested, charged and deported to Australia. As soon as he got there, he wrote to the man he had deprived and told him where he could find his property. Chapman was a skilled leatherworker who set up in business in Australia. Many years later he came back to visit his relatives in the area, an extremely prosperous man. He was the great uncle of Maurice Chapman who worked for us and who told me the story.

Poaching is now a shadow of its former self. Some still goes on, but not as a way of life or the supplement to people's incomes it used to be. The deliberate introduction of myxomatosis, and before that, gassing by farmers, has eliminated the larger part of the rabbit population, which was the bread and butter of the poacher. Pheasants were more the luxury end of the market, but, without the constant supply of rabbits, the whole game was not worthwhile.

There are one or two families in Chesham still supplementing their diet with the occasional trout from the River Chess, or the occasional pheasant, but nothing on the organized scale that there used to be. With access to the countryside now made legal by Act of Parliament, the offence of trespass has virtually disappeared. The lack of personal need, in the form of poverty, and leisure time divided into Continental holidays, has succeeded where generations of magistrates, gamekeepers, police and the whole Establishment failed. The industrial worker of Chesham has got rid of his ferrets and gone on holiday to the Costa Brava.

You can now go for a week through the woods and fields of the Chiltern countryside without ever seeing a local walking, without seeing any sign of life at all except the people working on the land, and the occasional group of urban ramblers, generally lost, unable to read their maps and walking through standing crops of corn. In the whole of Chesham, there are hardly any ferrets now or lurcher dogs which were kept entirely for catching rabbits. They were the safest way of catching rabbits because you could be on the road or on the footpath and could send your dog in pursuit of one. A lurcher couldn't be caught by any human being, certainly no keeper. He would bring the rabbit back to you without your having strayed off the public highway.

Far more people wandered about the countryside and walked farmers' land in the old days. The arrival of the car has had much more effect on people's habits in this way than any enforcement of the law against trespass ever had. Then everybody felt they had a God-given right to walk wherever they pleased, no matter that the notice said — 'Trespassers will be Prosecuted' — or what the law said. This was certainly the attitude I grew up with. Farmers would get infuriated at the sight of trespassers and would sometimes prosecute them. Rarely did they find it worthwhile because already the fines for this offence had gone down to minimal proportions, and it certainly did not stop people trespassing. Nowadays, people do not get out of their cars anyway.

It is a very short step from nicking a few turnips, a few potatoes or a bit of fruit, poaching rabbits, or taking trout out of the River Chess, when you know it is against the law — a very short step from that to another offence which I think is fairly prevalent in the countryside. This is stealing by finding. The modern joke about falling off the back of a lorry has a fairly firm basis in tradition in the countryside. Anybody unwise enough to leave their tools lying about inevitably lost them. This included council workmen and authorities of all sorts. Many farmworkers had access to new crowbars and hammers when people started laying electric power lines across the country. They kept turning up on our farm and when I asked where they came from, I was always faced with a perfectly blank stare: 'I found them lying about in the field and didn't know who they belonged to.'

Of course, it was always known whose they were. An extension of the same attitude, an extreme extension, was the case where I was short of harness on the farm and some turned up on one of my horses. The man who had taken it said, 'Well, there's plenty where that came from, and they won't miss it.' I had not got enough harness, whereas my neighbour had plenty, but I had to insist that it was taken back after dark. I could not inform on the chap who had taken it for my benefit. This was the relaxed and casual attitude to property. The same people would not have dreamed of breaking into a neighbour's house and stealing; in this way, they were more honest.

STEALING BY FINDING

Daffy Scott: September 1934

They called him Daffy Scott. I've no idea why. I never knew what his job had been and I never heard of him doing any work of a sort normally recognized as such. In an age and in a community where not to work was considered a terrible thing, I don't think anybody could have criticized him. First of all, there was something wrong with one of his hands. He kept it wrapped up all the time in a white cloth. As a child I was told he suffered from something called 'chalk hand'; I didn't ever find out what it was and I've never heard of it since. Perhaps he got some relief from the Parish, or help from his family, or perhaps he had money of his own; but he seemed to get his main income from what he found in the countryside. Every day of the year he walked endlessly around the fields (and nobody turned him off), round the lanes, looking up and down the hedges. In the early part of winter he was said to make his living by catching sleepers. A sleeper is a dormouse and they are not easy to find, but he apparently found enough to sell to pet shops in London to make a contribution towards his living.

Later in the winter, every time the hunt was out he would station himself at strategic points where there were gates that he knew some of the city dwellers out hunting would be afraid to jump but would rather that their fellow hunters thought they had jumped. When they arrived at the gates he would very quickly open them, let them through, and shut them again and they would give him a coin for saving them from the embarrassment of not being up to the job. Somehow, although he didn't walk very quickly, he would manage to intercept the hunt in several places on the same day and pick quite a bit up. Of course, that was only once or twice a week. The rest of the time it was just the dormice.

I don't know what he did in the spring. He still kept walking around so he must have found something to do or something to pick up, but then in the late summer he came into his own again. He always knew where the mushrooms were and you could see him walking slowly back to Chesham carrying a large bag of mushrooms every day of the week when there were any to find. It was in connection with his mushroom picking that I ran up against him, so to speak, face to face — the only time.

As I said, nobody minded him wandering around their farms and I didn't and I've never felt possessive about things wild on my land, but I was courting my wife at the time, who lived in Chesham, a town girl. She told me that both she and her mother were particularly fond of mushrooms, proper wild mushrooms and, in order to convince her what a beautiful farm I had and what marvellous mushrooms it grew, I went out one evening with a very large basket to pick a very large number of mushrooms to take to Florence and her mother.

I went in the top of the most likely field where I knew there would be masses of mushrooms. Just disappearing out of the bottom gate was Daffy Scott with a great big sack, which I suspected was full of mushrooms. I realized that he would have taken them all and my desire to impress my girlfriend overcame my socialist instincts and awakened my capitalist ones. They were my mushrooms, and he'd taken them. I rushed down after him, caught up with him and said, 'I want those mushrooms.'

He said, quite politely, 'You know, Mr Harman, they're not cultivated, I've as much right to them as you have.'

Just at that moment I didn't agree and I took the bag out of his hand and tipped them on the ground and I said (slightly recovering my normal conscience), 'You pick up half and I'll pick up half, then we'll be sharing what's come of its own accord, what's grown wild in my field.' He seemed to accept my logic; I never ran against him again.

You don't find people like Daffy nowadays, making their living in a simple way out of what they find in the countryside. Perhaps there's not quite so much to find. There are very few dormice about, they are a protected species. They lived mostly in the hedges which have now been so much cut down and trimmed; I've never found one living wild in the whole of my life. Catching them must have been a special skill.

Joe Bennett

When I first started farming, I employed a man called Joe Bennett who was an expert at stealing by finding. When we just grew things for home consumption, the fact that, like everybody else he helped himself to a few potatoes, a few turnips, did not really matter. When we started growing vegetables for sale and he helped himself to a whole bag of about forty pounds of peas which he or somebody else had been paid to pick, it was rather more serious. Although I knew he had taken it, he would deny it with a perfectly straight face and nothing could be proved.

A few weeks later, we started buying butter wholesale and selling it on our milk rounds along with our own milk. One day a whole box of butter disappeared and Joe, of course, was the first suspect. I got him cornered and accused him of having taken the butter. I pointed out that, if he brought it back, nothing further would be heard about it. With a perfectly straight face he said he had taken no butter. 'I have never taken anything in my life except them few peas,' he said, thereby admitting what he had so recently denied. So I had to keep a very sharp eye on what he was doing.

Then I got married. Joe saw in my marriage a golden opportunity for considerably expanding his stealing by finding. He volunteered to get up early and bring me and my wife a cup of tea to our bedroom at just after five o'clock. He knew that, when you are first married, your bed is very attractive and you do not want to get out of it, but a cup of tea helps. Joe knew I'd fall for it and it entitled him to walk through the house. He would never take anything of great consequence but if my wife left a packet of cigarettes about, there would be a few gone. There were fewer packets of tea, there was a little less sugar — a little less of everything — never enough to make a fuss about but a valuable supplement to Joe's income. He knew the luxury of a cup of tea in bed would never allow me to get up early enough to catch him.

He continued in this way for the whole of the three years he worked for me. I never sacked him; he went to a better job. In many ways he typified the attitude of the countryman: what falls in your path, you take. You use no violence and you do not overdo it — you just take a little bit of anything that comes your way. You would not dream of breaking into anybody's house or opening their door without their permission, but when you got permission to walk through the house, it was all quite different. It was just like walking in a field where things were really there to be taken.

CHILTERN MAN

partly an invention, but so was Piltdown man.

For me, the people of the area in which I live had a special character. They seemed in many ways different from the rest of the population in England. I call them, collectively, Chiltern man. Perhaps Chiltern man, like Piltdown man, never really existed, but more likely — as with Cro-Magnon man — he is now extinct, although traces remain. His decline is due to the fact that areas that were inhabited in my lifetime with real country people are now populated by immigrants from other areas — what Betjeman described as Metroland — and the local accent is now completely watered down.

Chiltern man's capital was Chesham and, for the most part, he made his living in agriculture or woodworking. His main characteristics over many centuries seem to have been extreme independence and a dislike of all authority; and although he had a close relationship with trees, since he was working with them, he had no respect for them.

The first example that seems to sum up the personality of Chiltern man is as far back as 1351 — one Sifrewast of Chesham who was in trouble for cutting down the Earl of Oxford's trees, in defiance of the Earl's orders. Medieval courts were surprisingly lenient and he seems to have just carried on even after later stealing thousands of cattle. Very much more recently, Hugh Batchelor — an ex-patriate Chiltern man, living in Kent — was sent to prison for cutting down protected trees in defiance of Maidstone Council, Kent County Council and Her Majesty's courts. Nothing much changes! After Hugh had come out of prison, my son, Dan, had occasion to talk to him about Dungrove Farm where Hugh was born and which we farm. His parting shot to Dan was: 'What are you going to do about all them bloody trees and hedges then?' But now Hugh seems to be a reformed character and has told the whole nation that he is planting trees.

Chiltern man's disrespect for authority led him to support the Protestant Reformation from an early stage. He didn't like the idea of priests telling him what to do and, even less, the idea of confessing. He was by nature a secretive man. For the most part, Chiltern man supported Parliament against the King. After all, the King tried to tax everybody and gave a lot of orders. John Hampden was a sort of gentlemanly Chiltern man, in the sense that he was a landed proprietor but, after all, he with his objection to the 'Ings' taxes — Charles's ship-money tax — almost started the English Revolution. He also signed the King's death warrant.

Emanating from the Chilterns and representing Wendover and the County of Buckingham in Parliament, Hampden fought for Cromwell in the Civil War and fought bravely at the battle of Edgehill. He was mortally wounded at Chalgrave Field, just outside Thame in the Aylesbury Vale, but insisted on being taken back to the Chiltern hills to die at his home in Hampden where he still lies.

I don't think Chiltern man worried over-much about the Restoration, any more than over Charles's death. After all, Cromwell's men had started giving orders a bit. Anyway it didn't change anything. Chiltern man embraced non-conformity with great enthusiasm and, by the middle of the 17th century, most were members of non-conformist churches. Priests and vicars tell you what to do but in non-conformist chapels if the minister doesn't do what you want him to you go and start a chapel of your own. And so, throughout the area, chapels proliferated in this period.

This time, the mid and late 17th century also produced the finest flowering of Chiltern man's attitudes. The best example I have come across to illustrate this involves a solicitor called William Child.

William Child was practising in Chesham, and had been a strong supporter of Parliament against the King. He was still practising under the Restoration. High Wycombe was a mainly Royalist town, always an establishment sort of place, and a verbatim report of William Child's blunt description of the burghers and magistrates of High Wycombe illustrates his attitude perfectly. This was a court record for August 1662 giving the reasons why an order was to be made for 'Outing Mr Willm Child Attorney from practising any longer in this Cort':

> And whereas the sayd Mr Child haveing severall tymes of late very insolently and uncivilly behaved himselfe towards the Mayor and Aldermen of this Burrough, As namely At A Court Dinner lately at the White Hart where in his discourse he gave to Mr Edward Bedder one of the Aldermen of this Burrough much undervaluing and slighting languige telling him in playne termes it should not be as he would have it.

The report then goes into details of further insults at the Courts General Sessions at the Guild Hall on April 10th, 1662:

> there being somme business of consequence to be discust that related to A matter in difference between the Burrough and the parish the sayd Mr Child being not retayned in the cause nor in the least concerned in it yet neverthelesse to shew how willing and how ready he was to doe the Burrough an Iniury did then and afterwards counsell the parishioners and side and take parte with them agaynst the Burrough and moreover deridingly in the open Hall did then say to the Major and Aldermen then presente 'You make your Charter A nose of Wax' and further did then publish and speake in a scoffinge manner severall scurrelous words tending to the reproach and discredit of the Mayor and Company in purpose to make men have them in derision.

An even more blatant example of his rudeness is then quoted from July 28th when he said to a Mr Richard Lucas:

> being a Justice of the peace and one of the Aldermen, in particular 'A Turd for you', and concerning the rest of the Court of Aldermen in generall, did say 'A Turd for them all', and (to show how slightly he valued his practise in this Court) afterwards further sayd that he cared not A fart whether ever he came into the Court any more or not; for all which severall misdemeanours, slovenly languige, maleepert caridge, and fanatick like deportment of the said Mr William Child it is resolved agreed uppon and ordered by the Mayor, Aldermen, and the Common Counsell of this Burrough that the said Mr Child shall not any longer continue An Attorny of this Court.

Child had won anyway because he didn't wish to continue practising in Wycombe as his practice was in Chesham, an ex-Parliamentary town.

To outsiders, Chiltern man has always appeared disagreeable and taciturn. The story is told of a 19th-century traveller journeying through the countryside in terrible weather on a dark stormy night and getting lost. He was looking for the village of Hawridge. He knocked on the window of a cottage and, mispronouncing the name of the place, said, when the door was reluctantly opened; 'Could you direct me to Horidge, please?' The door was slammed in his face with the announcement: 'I've never 'eard of it.' The traveller was, it transpired, already in the village of Hawridge, but the local thought he should have known how to pronounce it.

Young Chiltern people normally mated after chapel, to which everybody went. While this was going on, the older women would meet and play their favourite game of slander. The game was played like this. Two or three ladies would sit around a teapot. One of them would think of something nice to say about a neighbour and state it. Thereat all the others would say something like, 'That's what you think.' And the winner would be the one who could imply the greatest slander without actually precisely saying anything. One round was then finished and the other women would think of something nice to say. The fellow players would again try to imply that it couldn't possibly be true and that something evil was hidden behind it.

Now almost all of this has gone. Chiltern man has been overwhelmed by people moving in from places like Harrow. Harry, a farmworker since before the First World War, was typical: he always described his rather large wife as "is bit of old fat bakin". When asked if he had ever been to London his reply was, 'Wort do oi wornt to go there for? There's plenty of mud and worrta dane over 'ear.' The new arrivals are of quite a different type.

A particular nasal accent like that of Harry's, which required a harsh rasping voice, was probably produced by the Chesham bitter beer, which has long since gone out of production, together with the local hard water. It has all gone, to be replaced by something which is a sort of ITV-mid-Atlantic cockney.

But, just occasionally, instances of the old Chiltern man and his bloody-mindedness reappear. Recently, for example, a lorry driver was loading his vehicle in a Chesham street one early morning. He was holding up the traffic and a queue built up comprised of commuters, anxious to get to work. They hooted their horns. Chiltern man took not the slightest notice. Eventually, a tall athletic-looking man got out of one of the cars and walked to the front and said, surprisingly politely under the circumstances, 'Would you mind moving so that we can get to work?'

'When I'm done,' was the answer.

Athletic man then said, 'Are you aware that I'm a police Inspector?'

'That's what they all say,' said Chiltern man, and continued with his work.

But, like William Child before him, Chiltern man had won, because the policeman could hardly take him to court, having thrown his rank about over such a minor matter. He would have looked unbelievably pompous, so he just wrote to the man's employer to get him suitably reprimanded.

ARTHUR'S TALE

Arthur was a hard-working man, and he had a poor little farm, with a spartan house on it. All during the years of the Depression he had a very hard time. He kept going one way or another, and stories abounded in the district about his behaviour and his carefulness with money. That's the way he had survived.

One of my more successful neighbours, I remember, said to me once, 'Arthur's a good fellow. Very hard-working chap; but when he comes to see you, don't let him stand in front of the fire. It's awful.' Farm work's dirty, so I knew what he meant.

But he had money, without a shadow of doubt. I remember him once asking me if he could have a lift to the sale of a farm and when we got there, he bid for the farm — prices were much lower then, we are talking about just after the war — he bid £10,000. He failed to buy it, even though it had sold for only another £500 above his offer. On the way home he said to me, 'Mr Harman, have you ever borrowed any money?'

'Yes, Arthur, I shouldn't have got very far if I hadn't. I have borrowed money all my life.'

'Well,' he said 'maybe I should have borrowed a bit from the bank, or something, and gone that bit more, because it was a good little farm, much better than mine.'

I said, somewhat incredulously, 'What do you mean?'

And then he said, 'Well, I put £10,000 in my wallet, which is all the money I'd got in the house and I thought that would be enough to buy it, but it wasn't quite enough, was it?'

I was amazed because I have never carried £10,000 in my life, or anything like it, and here he was, looking very, very scruffy with £10,000 in his wallet.

And then there was the story about him and his brother Harry going up north to buy some sheep. Harry was a great big man, whilst Arthur was small and thin. Late in the afternoon, after they'd bought the sheep and arranged for them to be sent on later, they got on the train in Carlisle for the journey home. They had a compartment to themselves so they lay down, one on each side, and took off their boots. Harry had to go into London and then get a train back to Chesham to get to his farm, whereas Arthur lived in the Berkhamsted area but hadn't realized yet that he could get off at Watford. They went to sleep.

In the middle of the night, Arthur woke up and somebody was shouting, 'Watford. Watford. Next stop Euston.' So he thought to himself, 'I might as well get out here and go back to Berkhamsted straight away on the first train.' So he grabbed his boots and jumped out on to the platform. The train drew out, going on to Euston, and Arthur proceeded to put on the boots, but they were his brother's boots. He got them on all right, but they were two or three sizes too large. The unfortunate larger brother got to Euston, with a pair of boots far too small for him, so he couldn't get them on. And the story goes that he had to walk in stockinged feet in pouring rain to St Pancras police station, to borrow a pair of boots from a friendly policeman, before he could get back home to Chesham.

When I first had a combine harvester — one of the earliest in the district — we used to go round and do what could be described as 'specialist' work for other people, and we went late in the season to harvest some clover seed for Arthur. Clover seed is very small and, by the pound, quite valuable. Our man finished just as it was getting dark and Arthur said, 'There's some of my seed left in that machine. I've got to clear it out before you go.' And the driver said, 'I'm not stopping here any longer. I'm going off home. There's nothing much left in there. You'll have to speak to the boss about it' (that was me).

The next morning, Arthur was on the phone: 'Your combine has got some of my clover seeds still left in it.'

Knowing how mean he was, I said, 'It'll only be a handful Arthur.'

'Still, it's my seed you know. I've got to have it.'

'Alright then,' I said, 'when we clean it out — which we shall during the winter — we'll keep every bit of the dust and seed inside and you can have it. Because you're right, it is yours.'

We didn't clean the machine out for many weeks; we were too busy with other things. And about once every week, Arthur rang up and said, 'Have you cleaned out that combine yet? Got my clover seed out?' And I had to say, 'Not yet.'

If he'd thought about it, it must have cost him in telephone calls pretty well as much as the seed was worth. And in the end, towards the end of November on a wet day, we cleaned out the machine and put the seed and the dust and everything from inside it into a little bag, and I took it down to Arthur.

'There's your seed.'

He looked a bit disappointed: 'I should have thought there would have been more than that.'

I had to say, 'Well, there wasn't.' And I gave him a bill for the work that we had done for him. He paid up — a little reluctantly, I thought.

Arthur had had one son by his first wife, and it was he who had taken his wife, when she was about to give birth, to the knacker, Mr Wing, in Chesham, for help because he was the only person he thought he could completely rely upon. I've gone into that story in *Seventy Summers*.

When Arthur's first wife died, and I hasten to add that it was nothing whatever to do with that incident, I happened to run against him. 'Now Mr Harman,' he said to me, 'if you're unlucky and you lose your wife, don't marry again — it's not the same thing at all. My first wife was a good 'un: she worked hard and never spent any money at all; I would never have survived otherwise. But my new wife, she's used to different things. Before she even moved in she made me put in all sorts of baths and basins and things in the house and change it all around.

'And then, she won't live off the farm the way we used to. I'd only been married a few days, and came in at breakfast time with an old hen that had fallen off the perch. It was a bit weak, but I don't think there was anything wrong with it. Anyway, it was dead so we might as well use it. I said to my missus, "This'll do us for dinner," and she looked quite upset and said, "I'm not eating a thing that might have died from some disease. In fact, If you're going to eat that, I'll go into town and get myself a steak." I thought that was terrible, a terrible extravagance; so I set about and plucked that old hen myself and I said to my boy, "We'll have this for dinner; that'll be alright."

'When I cooked it, it was real good; in fact halfway through the meal I had to say to my boy, "Steady on, it'll easy do us two meals you know, and I don't know what it died of, so don't you eat too much of it".

'And there was my wife, eating steak all the while, which had cost a lot of money.'

LUCK MONEY

Farming is a business, at least in the sense that it is run by private people to make profit, and to make a living. The funny thing is that people in other businesses and other professions who have money imagine they can step straight into farming and do well. This has always been so: right through the Depression, businessmen would say, 'It's only farmers' bad organization that causes them to be in difficulties. If you applied proper business methods, it would be alright.'

A great idea in those days was to follow a businessman on a farm. He generally equipped it with the best modern machinery, repaired all the buildings, did the roads, cut the hedges and then got fed up with losing money in about three years. If you could follow him in the tenancy then you were made for life; you got all these advantages for practically nothing, they were never taken account of in the rent. No building repairs to do, no road repairs to do, for years and years and years; even, perhaps, no hedging to do for years. Lots of artificial fertilizers had been wasted by the businessman on the land, so the land was in a high state of fertility.

It is quite fun to watch these people when they go into farming, at stock sales. They have an idea that if you buy the most expensive bull, and mate him with the most expensive cow, you are bound to get the best progeny. Of course it is not like that at all, but you see them at sales and they don't start bidding until the price is quite high. The real pros around the ring just need to help each other and get their animals started beyond a certain point, and then the businessmen will buy them. Of course it doesn't work out. They don't breed the best progeny; there is much more to cattle breeding than just the price of the first animals you buy.

Another class of person who is always trying to go into farming, probably with even less qualifications than the businessman, is retiring army officers, maybe coming from fairly wealthy families with a bit of capital that has accumulated during their service period, with a pension as well. During the Depression they generally finished up just trying to make a living by letting out horses, if they were near enough to a town, or breeding horses in the vain hope of making a living that way. Mostly it didn't last very long.

I have, of course, to confess that my father was a businessman going into farming, and it isn't just loyalty that makes me say he was different. He was. He thought about it for such a long time and tried it out on a small scale for twenty years before he really got started, and I am sure that if he had lived long enough he would have made a brilliant success of it, far better than me. His great-grandfather had been a farmer in Sussex; maybe something had been passed down unconsciously.

I had a personal experience of someone from outside farming, with money, making a complete ass of himself. It was during the middle of the war, and I was rung up one night by somebody I knew who asked if I'd care to go to Scotland and buy a whole herd of cattle for him, commission and expenses included of course. I was hard up at the time and I jumped at the opportunity. Arrangements were made for the client to come down and see me. He walked around my herd and expressed himself highly delighted with the quality of the animals. I don't think he really knew much about it. I was pleased and he was pleased. And yet, his adventure into farming proved to be very, very expensive.

At first, I only knew that he wanted me to go with him to Scotland and choose a very large number of Ayrshire cattle; he was going to establish a milking herd in East Anglia. He told me that he had been invalided out of the army, a captain, just about the same time as he had inherited a considerable sum of money from his grandfather. At that time he had met an old school friend, with a little experience of farming, who had said, 'You should buy yourself a farm. Now, in wartime, it's a good thing.' They had gone to the local town, bought the local newspaper and found an auction advertised for two days later with a large farm with a very big house. The house was semi-derelict; that didn't put him off. They had duly gone to the sale; he had bought this farm, lock, stock and barrel, really without any plans of how to use it, except that he was of Scottish extraction and wanted a herd of Ayrshire cattle.

In the first instance he didn't invite me to go to see the farm, otherwise I think I would have panicked. I arranged to meet him at Euston Station and we went up to Glasgow and thence to Castle Douglas in south-west Scotland, and then we got a lift across the hills with a breeder to Ayrshire. And everywhere we went, we bought cattle. We bought more than I wanted to. The Captain would go into a farmer's premises and be shown a bunch of heifers. I would start to pick out one or two and he would say, 'Are these good cattle?' And I would say: 'Oh yes, on the whole.'

So he would more or less buy the lot. And in Castle Douglas market where the habit of giving luck-pennies, that is, money back to buyers, is very common, I as the bidder buying these large numbers for my friend ended up with the most enormous luck-penny that I have ever heard of anybody getting. But I did my best for him, and I think we bought good cattle. He then said, 'Come on, we'll go back to Glasgow, and we'll go to the Central Hotel and we'll get as good a meal as you can get in the middle of war.' And we did just that.

It wasn't until we were in the train the following morning, on the way back to Euston, that I started asking him about the arrangements for receiving the cattle. The vendors had been instructed to put them on rail within a few days. In those days transport was mostly by rail. The auctioneers in Castle Douglas market assured us that they would definitely put them on a train. In those days cattle were both fed and milked by the railway company in transit. Somewhere, en route from Glasgow to Euston — and the trains were very slow in those days — I said to him, 'What feed have you got laid on for these cattle when they arrive?'

He looked at me quite blankly: 'There are several grass fields.'

'But this is February,' I said, 'and in the winter months cattle have to be fed with stored food — hay, silage, grain, and what have you.'

'Nobody told me.'

'Did you ask anybody?'

'Anyway, there are great stacks of straw there, surely that will do?'

'It might help,' I said, 'but it won't exactly do.' Then I added, 'What's the labour situation like? Have you got people who are used to milking?'

'No. But there's nothing to that, is there? They've all worked on farms all their lives; they must know how to milk.'

I pointed out that it was an arable area and they might well not know how to milk. By the time we got to Euston, some of my fears were rubbing off on him and his confidence was oozing away.

'What have I got to do?'

'Well,' I said, 'I'll do one thing. I'll make some emergency arrangements in Chesham to accept the animals from Castle Douglas. Some will need milking and those that are about to calve will have to be calved. And we'll ask all the private vendors to hold their cattle until further orders.'

He seemed fairly satisfied. 'When the cattle do arrive, you had better come down and sort things out. I'll pay you, of course.'

When I had asked him about the milking, he had said he was installing a milking machine. 'When will the installation be finished?' I asked. He hadn't the least idea.

I suppose three or four weeks had passed, it's a long time ago so I can't remember exactly, when I got a message that the cattle on my place could be sent forward, and the others called for from Scotland. At least he had organized something.

I had bought him two or three bulls because there were a large number of cattle. One bull had caused us quite an adventure because at the same time as contacting me, the Captain had written to somebody in Scotland who advertised Ayrshire cattle. This man was a well-known dealer and he considered that he had sold a bull to my friend. I was instructed to go and approve it. The man was angry at the possibility that it might not be approved and I remember we had a heavy night's drinking in the Temperance Hotel at Castle Douglas, trying to pacify him — with whisky brought in, of course. And the next morning, I imagine with a terrible hangover, he drove us over the hills to Dumfries and Ayrshire, over frozen roads and I remember being frightened out of my life. It was a perfectly good bull.

By the time I got to the Captain's farm, all my fears had returned. I was met at the local station by him and taken, not to the farm, but to an ordinary country house a couple of miles away, which he had purchased because his wife didn't care for the farmhouse. Hardly surprising, because it was nearly in ruins and very, very big. He confided in me that he had 'got a bit of a problem' because petrol was rationed — this was in the middle of war, remember — and the water at the farm was pumped with a petrol engine. Unfortunately he had already used most of his month's allocation in going backwards and forwards from the farm to his house.

I stayed, I believe, three nights, and got the milking organized as best I could, doing some of it myself to set a good example. Fortunately not many of the cows were yet in milk and some of the old men on the farm could milk, after a fashion. Meantime, the engineer from the milking-machine company was installing the plant — going slow because he obviously rather fancied the farm manager's wife; I didn't blame him. After three days we got some sort of order, some sort of routine for these largely unskilled arable workers to do the milking. The milking machine was finally installed. The Captain had gone to the local town and got himself an additional ration of petrol. I advised him to tell the people handing out the petrol coupons all the facts, as they would understand that he couldn't live in the enormous half-ruined farmhouse.

Still a lot of animals left to calve, with a major proportion of the Victorian buildings on this farm designed for horses: loose boxes, with windows very high up, with bars over them. These were to lead to the next disaster.

Meanwhile, I had gone home, hoping that everything would go well. I had received a cheque for my services to date, quite satisfactory as I was hard up. And then, one morning, a panic-stricken captain came on the phone: 'You'll have to come down again! There's a hoodoo on this place! The cows are committing suicide left, right and centre. The knacker is here positively every day!'

I arrived late in the evening, too late to get to the farm, so I was taken to the house again and given a nice dinner, cooked by the wife, a charming, oriental lady who seemed very sensible. During the course of dinner my friend started on again about the hoodoo and the wife said, 'There's no such thing as hoodoo, forget it!'

'But really, you'll see tomorrow morning,' he insisted. 'They have committed suicide.'

My friend is slightly given to exaggeration, I found. In fact what had happened, was that two or three of the animals, confined to those dark, Victorian loose boxes and needing to find somewhere to calve, had jumped up to look out of the window. They had got their horns caught in the bars and had hung themselves. It wasn't suicide, it was accidental death and in fact there had been only two; but others had attempted the exercise, most getting away with just breaking a horn off. In those days cattle still had horns on them; it couldn't happen today because everybody takes the horns off as soon as they start growing. Again, I sorted things out as best I could, and arranged that the cows that were about to calve should be put in different places.

The labour on the farm was, I think, quite happy to talk with me because I at least knew something about what I was doing, whereas the boss knew very little, or nothing.

I heard no more for six months, nor had I in fact been paid for the last baling-out session. But this may have been a consequence of my letter telling him that he should never have gone into farming in the first place and that a fool and his money are soon parted. However, six months later, I got a letter enclosing a cheque. Right throughout the whole proceedings he proved to be a dead honest man. There was something very nice and very innocent about him. And with the cheque was a letter saying 'Please come and see me again. I've just bought another farm.'

My heart sank — some people never learn. Hadn't the folly of him going into farming got through to him yet? Had he doubled the folly? So I went down there again, and said, 'What's all this about?'

'Well,' he said, 'it's a very good farm. Everybody tells me it's the best farm in the area and it's bang next door, so I bought it.'

'You must be rolling in money,' I said.

'Well, as a matter of fact, I put an advertisement in The Times to say that I needed money to buy a farm, and farms are such good security now that several people offered me the money and I took two lots. One on the first farm, and one on the second.'

I think I politely refrained from saying, 'You are absolutely mad' because he was such a nice chap. I went to see the new farm, an old-fashioned place, with a very sensible old-fashioned foreman, a large number of horses — although tractors were already quite numerous in the countryside — on good land, and they were doing the job perfectly. I merely said: 'Leave that foreman alone and he'll probably make money for you. He knows what he's at. And when you know what you're at, maybe then you can start altering things, but leave him alone, he's alright.' Hopefully he did.

A further six months passed by and, eight o'clock one morning, the phone rang. It was the Captain: 'I want to sell all my cows! The men in this part of the world don't know anything about cows, they're not doing well.' He was half right about that.

It just so happened that I knew somebody in Bucks who was just starting into milk production, and I rang him up. 'George, if you care to come down to this place, there are a large number of cattle which were very good when they were bought. They may have been neglected. You might get a bargain.'

George, who worked on a large scale, together with his manager, stockman and I, went down to the Captain's place. We were shown the cattle in a casual sort of way, nobody seemed to have kept records of when they should calve or anything like that. It was a bit of a muddle but on the whole they looked quite healthy. A number of them were sorted out and George said, 'I'll give you £11,000 for the lot.'

The Captain, apparently not listening to the other party said, 'I made up my mind when I got up this morning, I wouldn't take less than £10,500.' Needless to say, George's cheque-book was out very, very quickly and the Scottish stockman said, 'Christ, look how I have to work for £500 and he's just thrown it away.' In fact the Captain's mind was on other things.

George, amongst other things, had a bacon factory which he had mentioned, and so the Captain started laying down the law about how he would go into pigs and have his own bacon factory. George's farm manager had mentioned that they were going in for herbage seeds, that is to say grass seeds, which were then quite profitable because they couldn't be imported from other countries, so the Captain announced that he would start seed growing and have his own seed farm.

I didn't hear anything from him then for quite a long while. I didn't get the remaining money owing to me, commission on that sale, and so on, for a great many years. But I had it in the end. From time to time during the next two or three years I would see letters, signed by the Captain, in the farming press, telling other farmers how they should run their businesses. How they should process what they grew, how, if they had pigs, they should have their own bacon factory; all the things we had heard before about seed sowing, seed cleaning — generally telling everybody else what they should do.

And then one day I had a letter from a firm of solicitors which said, 'In the matter of So-and-So, the creditors are asked to hold their hand,' or words to that effect, meaning not to sue, 'and they will be paid in the end from our client's estate.' I didn't bother to argue about it nor did I go to the ensuing creditors' meeting. But in the end, after many years, I was, to my great surprise, paid in full with interest at proper bank rates. I was astonished when the money came, and, of course, delighted.

Maybe a fool and his money are soon parted, but at least he was a very, very, honest fool, as were his family trust who in the end paid all.

TRAVELLING MEN

Gypsies, tinkers, didicoys — people who wander, what the French would just call 'nomad' — have been with us in the Chilterns for centuries. There was a mention in Elizabethan times in the church registry in Chesham of a man from Watford killed by tinkers at Bellingdon. When you think now how Bellingdon is, a commuting suburb of Chesham, nearly all built up, it seems slightly bizarre. What was this chap from Watford doing there, anyway? Was he walking or was he on a horse? No details were written. Just 'killed by tinkers', and no particulars of what the authorities did to the tinkers; whether they caught them, hung them, imprisoned them, or just forgot about it. Tinkers are not normally mentioned in things like church registers, because they didn't register their children, and when, in the 19th century, schools became compulsory, gypsy children were not, at first, made to go. I suppose school attendance officers couldn't catch them because they kept moving.

When I first came on the scene there seemed to be a lot of gypsies about; most of them quite prosperous, dealing in horses, going to various fairs, keeping their horses on the grass on commons; living in caravans, a good many of which looked really very smart — well-painted and bright and cheerful. They never stayed anywhere long enough to annoy anybody much, it was just accepted that they came and went. Perhaps a couple of caravans would settle on a tiny bit of land like Lye Green; they would hobble their horses — that is to say, tie their front legs together, in a way that would be illegal nowadays (allegedly cruel to the horses) — and stay there until all the grass on the green had been eaten. Councils in those days didn't bother to cut grass on village greens.

Then they'd move on. Or on larger commons, like Ley Hill, there would sometimes be quite a gathering of them in advance of an event like Chesham Fair, where they would come and buy and sell horses, right in the middle of Chesham, in the Broadway. The same thing happened in other towns.

Horses don't leave anything much that's untidy behind, a little horse dung soon disappears and it's a natural thing that nobody bothers about anyway. The gypsy women cut hazelwood from the hedges — which caused a certain amount of damage — and made clothes pegs which they sold around the houses. At a different, economically lower level, there were others who went round singly or in pairs, presumably husband and wife, with some sort of a barrow, sharpening knives or mending pots and pans. They were the ones that were originally known as tinkers. That's all changed nowadays, when large bands of Irishmen are labelled as tinkers. They don't mend any pots and pans.

During Victorian and Edwardian times, quite a lot of gypsy families settled down and became part of the normal community. There are a number of families in Chesham who originated that way, and they soon became much like anybody else, although they sometimes retained their ancient traditions. When a gypsy died, they habitually burnt his caravan, sometimes just his bed. Within relatively recent years the mother of a well-known businessman in the area died and some of the employees were instructed to take her bed and burn it on a bit of common land, according to the gypsy customs with which she had been brought up. A few of the better-off ones, what one might describe as 'horse-drawn' gypsies, used to settle on farms during the harvest season and help with the work, then move on when it was done, leaving behind little mess. They were there by agreement and I suppose had some sense of responsibility towards the farmer.

The general population was always slightly suspicious about them. There is the traditional song village children used to sing, 'My mother said I never should play with the gypsies in the wood,' a sort of mad idea that gypsies kidnapped ordinary children. Heaven knows why they should want to do that, because they generally had plenty of their own. Up to the second world war, most of the gypsies were probably genuine Romanies; many spoke their own language. Only later were they increased in number and diluted by simple drop-outs taking up the gypsy way of life — people that we in Buckinghamshire call didicoys — and vast numbers of tinkers from Ireland, who leave appalling mess behind when they move on.

During the 'twenties and 'thirties, a few gypsies settled in semi-permanent camps. Down Long Lane, Bovingdon, there was such a camp, a whole lot of caravans grouped together, a sort of tiny village. And there they manufactured various simple things which they sold at fairs, and they still dealt in horses although they were beginning to deal in lorries and cars as well. I ran against them two or three times — their name was Smith. In about 1938 a young gypsy man came to me and asked if he and his wife could stay in my field for a bit. I saw

no harm in letting him camp on the stubble field and he seemed a very nice young man, so I gave him permission and he settled down, dragged in his caravan and was there with his wife and some children. Within days the head of the clan, old Mr Smith, was along:

'You must send that lot home.'

'Why should I?' I asked.

'If you don't send that lot home, I shall get the sanitary man on them.' In those days there were no planning officers, the only chap was the sanitary man and it would appear that while the gypsies had some arrangements which satisfied the authorities in their settled village at Bovingdon, in my field there weren't any. I refused to put any pressure on them but in the end they went back to the family in Bovingdon.

That connection was to prove, a bit later, quite useful. During the war, in the middle of one winter, my Suffolk Punch horses of which I was very proud, disappeared. They disappeared during the night and it was like some Victorian melodrama. It was snowing heavily and no tracks could be found. I reported it to the police and nothing happened and at the end of a week or two the police said to me, 'I'm sorry; you had better accept that they were stolen for slaughter and are dead by now, and will never be found. There's a lot of it going on.'

I was desperate: they represented a whack of my capital, and I was proud of them anyway. I had an idea and went along to the gypsy encampment at Bovingdon, told them I'd lost my horses, and asked if they had heard anything about them. They thought I was accusing them of stealing. I wasn't and made that clear. Then I said, 'If you hear of any large, ginger-coloured horses somewhere where they ought not to be, just let me know and I will give you £5.'

At the time, I was standing at the door of old Mr Smith's caravan and there was a mirror inside, and in the mirror I could see a swarthy old lady making boiled sweets, which I imagine they were going to sell around a fair. I don't know where they got the ingredients from because sugar was rationed at that time. I suppose they might have had a ration of some sort, I really don't know. But while I was talking she, unaware that I could see her in the mirror, was nodding her head. She knew something. It was really quite extraordinary. Later that day there was a clattering on the lane by my farm and two young gypsy men came along, bringing my horses with them.

'Where did you find them?' I said.

'In a field, never you mind.'

I tried to ask them who had had them, but not a word could I get, except 'It wasn't us and it wasn't any gypsies, and it wasn't any of our people.'

I naturally told the police I had found them and their response was: 'Well, you're lucky. It's no good us asking any questions either, the only effect would be that you'd never get any help from them again.'

I'm pretty certain that the Smiths hadn't taken them. At home, we felt we'd got to celebrate in some way, and in the middle of the war very little was obtainable, but I did manage to get hold of a bottle of Benskins cheap rum. There was nothing to go with it, except the children's orange juice and Ribena; and the evacuee we had at the time, the English wife of a serving Norwegian naval officer, and I got, I'm afraid, a bit drunk on this mixture. My wife just couldn't face it, but we had to celebrate somehow or other.

Years and years afterwards, I heard a rumour that the Suffolks had been stolen by a man (not a gypsy), who was running a regular and very profitable black-market meat business during the war, and he was keeping the horses in a field away from the road until the hue-and-cry, such as it was, was off; he would then have slaughtered them and nobody would have been any the wiser. Except that the gypsies were wiser; they knew what was going on all around them and were perfectly prepared to earn an honest pound or two out of somebody else's dishonesty.

When old Mr Smith eventually died, a very old man, I'm told that gypsies came from miles around to see his caravan being burnt. All this traditional way of life, dealing in horses, selling clothes-pegs, has been destroyed by modern civilization. The sort of horses they dealt with are no longer required. Fairs still go on, but I suppose on a rather reduced, different basis. Wooden clothes pegs, carved out of one piece are a thing of the past. So we, the general community, have destroyed their way of life. In addition to that, we have done things like make their children go to school, and all of this has created quite a different, hostile atmosphere towards travelling people.

Gypsies moved with the times, going quite naturally from horse-dealing to car-dealing, dealing in second-hand cars at the bottom end of the market, breaking them up, on the roadside because that is where they live. Leaving behind the bits that were unsaleable, which makes an awful mess, and that brought them face to face with the authorities. And the mere fact of this made both sides more hostile. Making the children go to school also caused trouble. The children were often rather dirty and they smelt; the respectable parents of children in the village schools started to complain, the authorities started to make the children wash when they got to school, and there was general hostility all round. My wife used to be chairman of the governors at Ley Hill School and had to settle endless trouble about washing the children before going to school each day.

By the 'fifties gypsies could no longer camp on farmers' land where they wouldn't have been so much trouble, because planning restrictions would have caused the farmer himself to be prosecuted for an unlicensed caravan site, and so, by the 'sixties and 'seventies there was an entirely different atmosphere. The gypsies, if still they were gypsies and not tinkers, had gathered into large bands, possibly for self-protection, leaving behind the most terrible mess all around the home counties. On one occasion there were seventeen caravans on a small bit of grass verge just next to our farm. They made an awful mess of the site and they left their rubbish about. They quarrelled and fought and everybody was hostile to them: hardly surprisingly. Eventually, the authorities — the police and the local council — cleared all these away and, by agreement with the authorities, I dug a ditch so they couldn't get back again.

I feel I was then blamed unfairly for what had happened to them, because a few nights later all the straw from that year's harvest on my farm, a huge quantity, went up in flames and nobody could explain it. I was returning home at the time and saw it from miles away. But it wasn't my fault that they had been moved on. Though I didn't like them being there, I didn't particularly want to get them moved, in fact I was quite sorry for them. But somebody, I suppose, had to be held responsible.

At that point, the authorities nationally felt something should be done, so councils were instructed to make sites available for them with washing facilities and toilets so they could move from place to place. A worthy objective with which no doubt some travellers co-operated but certainly not all. Quite a few took out the copper fixtures of the toilets and sold them almost immediately. A local council official told me of one occasion where they'd made a brand new site and there were a lot of gypsy caravans on it; the gypsies left, together with most of the equipment from the lavatories and wash-houses. The council put the things right again and another lot of gypsies arrived, and he thought he would go and see how they were getting on. He went up early one morning and almost everything had disappeared, but there was a large lorry leaving, stacked high with pieces of pipe and stuff. He stopped it and a big, burly Irishman leant out of the cab and said, 'Oh Sir, they left the most terrible mess. I've cleared it up. Will you give me £10 for my work?' Quite unashamed!

These people are living on the proceeds of our wasteful society. They are making a living out of what the rest of us use and discard. As well as breaking up old cars, some of them, with or without permission, go totting on rubbish dumps and collect things which the general public have thrown away, in sufficient quantities to sell. It's a far cry from the rather romantic, and certainly harmless, trekking around the country with horses, leaving nothing more noxious than a bit of horse dung behind. And it's not popular. But what else could they have done?

Even more sad, perhaps, is the complete disappearance of the knife grinders, the scissor sharpeners and people like that who were always at a low economic level, a lot of them living under a crude tent somewhere in a hedge between visits to different villages. One in our area used to be known as 'the black gypsy', a very swarthy man who, with his wife, went round from door to door with a barrow offering quite politely to grind your knives, sharpen your scissors. Their living has gone competely and you will still occasionally see them around, looking drab and pathetic and living on even smaller quantities of waste things which they collect from the roadside where they were dumped, and manage to sell.

BRICKWORKS

Bricks have been made around Ley Hill for a very long time, four hundred years at least, and in the beginning pots and pans were made as well, and at various times roof tiles. Hence there are several little places in the area called 'Tylers Hill'.

Bricks used to be made on every patch of the Chilterns where there was enough clay without any stones in it. There were literally dozens of brickworks up to the outbreak of war; now I think there are four left at the most, those with the biggest reserves of clay, or those owned by the people who had enough capital to install at least some modern machinery.

The local clay makes extremely high-quality bricks if it's burnt right, but it has always been a skilled business. The process can't be industrialized in the way that it can be with the Bedfordshire kilns, but of course the method has changed a bit — with some machinery used and gas for burning the bricks.

When I first remember them, the bricks were dried in the open air under wooden covers called 'hacks', exactly as they would have been in Roman times — long rows, set out waiting for the summer air to dry them — and when they were dry they were burnt in relatively crude kilns using, in my time, coal but originally wood. Somebody sat up all night to keep the fire burning around and inside the kiln.

It used to be a seasonal job. They would dig the clay in the winter, and make and burn the bricks in the summer because they had no means of getting the clay dry enough to burn in the winter. People talk about baking bricks — they are not baked, they are burnt. These days the clay has coke breeze mixed with it to assist in the burning; originally it was sawdust or straw or something similar, and when the clay was very dry it would burn, with the coal all around it to keep the heat up.

The work of digging the clay in the winter was done at a fairly leisurely pace because there was plenty of time. Once the making season started in the spring, everybody worked all the hours there were, piece work, being paid by the thousand for what they made. It used to be said that the tile-makers of Tylers Hill, however heavy they were in the spring, had lost so much weight by the end of the making season that they could get through their tile mould, which was only something like 11″ by 8″. Takes a bit of believing, but that's what was said.

In 1987 when a new house was being built at Ley Hill, a Tudor tile kiln was uncovered on a spot where they had also made earthenware pots out of the local clay. I like to think it belonged to a family who appear frequently in the church register of Chesham in Tudor times, a family called Overstreet. I became fascinated by the fact that there were many of them in the register described as 'brickmaker' or 'potter', and that all of a sudden in the early 17th century the whole lot disappeared — no further Overstreets registered in the area whatsoever. It so fascinated me that when travelling in other parts of Britain, I have looked in the local telephone directories for the name; but I have only ever found one Overstreet, in Bedford. I felt like ringing him up, but I didn't. But none in the London telephone directory, none in north country telephone directories; where had they all gone? It remained a complete mystery to me, and I wondered if they had all changed their names. There was one in the early 17th century with an entry after him in the parish register, 'alias Potter', so he at least had changed his surname to his occupation. This didn't seem likely for the whole clan, but they had disappeared all the same.

And then, in 1983, when I was in America staying with my daughter in Alabama, I told her about my preoccupation with the Overstreets. 'Well, I know a Miss Overstreet,' she said. 'I'll ring her up.'

Miss Overstreet was a very old lady living on her own. 'Do you know where you come from?' my sister asked her.

'Virginia.'

They talked for some time but her reply to my daughter's question excited me. 'What did your family do?'

'Oh, they made bricks and tiles.'

Virginia was an English colony. For me the story was complete. The whole family of Overstreets from Ley Hill and Botley, near Chesham, had gone to America to establish a brick-making industry there and had left behind the remains of their pot kiln at Ley Hill. At least, that is what I like to think.

The bricks made in the area are very popular with architects. They are a nice mixed colour — nothing dull or uniform about them. They like to specify them for new houses of the more expensive type. They are demanded too by the planners for certain parts of the main streets of Old Amersham and Beaconsfield. Everybody likes them, but nobody likes to see them being made. When the four brickfields currently in working occupation run out of clay, and somebody wishes to start making them somewhere else, the locals will be up in arms. 'No industrial development in this area! No dirty old brick kilns in this area!'

And what will they do then for their fancy bricks to match up the old buildings?

QUEEN VICTORIA'S JUBILEE

I didn't know the village of Brill until the mid 'forties, though of course I knew where it was. I'd passed within sight of it on my way to Banbury market via Bicester, through the flat boggy plain where Oxfordshire and Buckinghamshire join, all of which until recent years was grassland, permanently green because it was too wet to plough. Whereas Brill, being one of a number of small hills standing out of the plain, always looked brown; possibly because the soil was lighter or it drained better and some of it had been ploughed, but brown it looked. As I went by, I always thought of it and the other small hills as looking like a herd of cows lying in a green meadow. Of course it has all changed now because the whole lot has been drained and it's all ploughed and it's all about the same colour. And if all those little hills, most of which are nameless and not proper hills like the Chilterns where my farm is, if they all look like cows, well Brill is the biggest so that's the bull, lying contented in a large green meadow looking over his rather smaller cows.

In the mid 'forties I suddenly got a request to go to Brill. I was the chairman of the local Labour Party and the boundary commissioners in their wisdom, or otherwise, had decided that the village of Brill,

instead of being part of the North Bucks constituency, should be added to the Aylesbury constituency. That was us, and we had to go and meet our new colleagues.

I'd heard a bit about it. The whole area had a strong radical tradition going right back, one could almost argue, to the Middle Ages. Hadn't Wycliffe been living over at Lugershall when he almost started the English Reformation? So I had heard that the people of the area had always been open to new ideas. The village of Brill itself was said to be a mixture of the normal village people, squires and farmers. There were quite a lot of old-fashioned radicals and a few Oxford dons, most of whom would be on our side anyway, at least at that time.

Anyway, with one or two friends, I duly went there one beautiful summer's evening and we set up on a bit of common land to introduce ourselves with a loudspeaker to the people of Brill. A few came out to listen; one of the Oxford dons stood at the back of the little group saying 'hear, hear' in a superior voice at appropriate moments. What I said was well enough received but most of them had obviously heard it before. The squires, the farmers, and those that did as they were told, had not come out to listen, nor did we expect them. And after we'd given a decent airing to the problems that might arise, and the hopes we had of co-operation in the forthcoming election, we decided to adjourn to the pub, of which there were several. In villages there is always just one pub favoured by each particular group, and there was one favoured by our group. Just as we were going off — and I was rather looking forward to a glass of beer because it was a warm evening and I had been the one doing the talking — a very old man plucked at my sleeve, and he said, 'Young man, I want to tell you a story.'

My heart sank, I had heard that sort of thing before. Everybody else would be drinking comfortably and I would have this old fellow telling me a long, and probably boring story. He said, 'I want to tell you the story of how we spoilt Queen Victoria's jubilee.' Well, it did at least sound different and I had to be polite because I had to work with them, so I stopped and all the others walked on, and he started.

'Well, it was like this you see, it was one of Queen Victoria's jubilees. I can't remember which one. The Squire called us all together in the village and he said, "It's Her Majesty's jubilee this summer, as I am sure you all know, and we shall have to celebrate as loyal subjects, and I suggest that we celebrate by having a fete and planting some trees on Brill common."

'Well, there was a lot of us radicals in the hall, nobody had asked us our opinion. We didn't bear the old woman any ill will but we didn't see why we should celebrate her anniversary by planting trees on Brill common where there had never been any before. (Highly progressive attitude that was!) Anyway, we didn't say anything at the meeting, there was no point, but when the meeting broke up we got together and we made our plans. Just quite quietly, just us radicals and we didn't tell anybody about it.

'Well, the day came. There were marquees up, there were sports and side-shows, and holes had been dug by the estate workers for the trees to be planted in, and the trees were there all ready. During the afternoon a little party approached the first hole, the Squire and the Lord Lieutenant of the County who was to plant the tree, with several other local dignitaries. They came to the hole and there was a radical sitting in the hole.

'Squire said, 'Get out, my man, so that his Lordship can plant the tree.' And the radical never said nothing, he just sat in the hole and said not a word, and because it was common land, they daren't move him, in fact they couldn't move him. So they moved to the next hole, and the same thing, another radical sitting in the hole, so they couldn't plant that tree either. And so it went on round all the holes that had been dug — a radical sitting in each one.

'Well, I was only a lad at the time, but I can remember that several of the parties' faces were getting very red by now and they were looking a bit embarrassed, and I heard Squire say, 'Well, let's go and have some tea. I'm sure they'll come to their senses, especially when the public houses open.'

'Well, as a matter of fact, most of the radicals were teetotallers anyway so opening pubs didn't make any difference. However, just like the rest of 'em, we wanted a cup of tea, so when they went off for their cup of tea, the radicals went off for theirs. And they came back quite quickly, hoping to get the ceremony over and then, in each hole, there was a radical's wife sitting. And the same thing happened as before. They never answered back. They were never rude or anything like that. They weren't that sort of people, but the radicals' wives wouldn't get out of the holes either, so the trees never did get planted.'

Now I don't know whether the story was true or not. It possibly isn't, it possibly is an old man's imaginings of some minor happening that occurred many, many years ago. But I do know that there are no trees growing on the Common at the point that he indicated to me, not to this day. So perhaps it was a triumph for Victorian radicalism.

The secret on all these occasions is to let whoever wants to talk to you do the talking, and never, never to join in yourself with any stories to silence them. On another occasion I was asked to go in a cottage of an elderly man who had been a supporter for very many years, and to introduce myself. I suppose I overdid it. I talked for rather a long time and he never told me any stories. All he did, when asked by the person who had introduced us if he would like to ask me any questions, was to hand me a teapot with two spouts saying; 'Have you ever seen anything like this before?' which made me think I had talked too much, and that is what he'd kept the thing for.

THE LAND GIRLS

It was the right sort of day for doing new things. Bright and sunny in the early summer and not too hot. We had grown sugar beet for the first time on any scale and we didn't really know much about it — at least I didn't. Old Will did; he came from Lincolnshire, where they had grown it always, but of course conditions were quite different there: it grew much more easily and was easier to hoe and keep clean, there weren't the stones to deflect you and make your life difficult.

We had realized we hadn't nearly enough labour to single the beet. Sugar beet has a horrible habit of growing up in tangled groups, two or three from each seed, and nowadays, to avoid having to thin them, the seeds are first broken down and pelleted so that they come up already arranged at intervals. In those days, however, you sowed the beet seed in a thick row, you chopped the row out into bunches with a hand hoe and somebody had to get down and disentangle clumps of beet into single plants. We bought a lot of new hoes for the new labour to use when it came. There were five regulars, including myself, on the farm and we had the milking to do twice a day and the horse work and very little time for all this extra hoeing. Some overtime in the evening, but not much during the day.

So I phoned the War Ag and asked for extra help. They said, 'Well, the men from the hostel at Chartridge' — they were Conscientious Objectors — 'they are all out. A pity, as some of them are pretty good. You'll have to have land girls. They're all new on the job and you'll have to teach them.'

And there they were that sunny morning; everything about them bright and new. They'd never worked on a farm before, we'd never had girls on the farm before. They had brand-new khaki overalls on, over bright green jumpers. They were carrying over their arms short overcoats of a deep fawn colour, rather like what senior army officers used to wear called 'British warms'. I don't know who had designed their outfits, but they looked lovely that morning, all bright and clean, all laughing; all, I expect, looking forward to something different.

Eight of them were dropped off at our place and the rest of the lorry load went smilingly on their way, talking animatedly to each other and obviously talking about us. I wonder what they expected to find on the farms?

I don't remember them all by name, but I do some of them. There was Hannah, a big, strong-looking girl, half Irish, from somewhere in the East End of London, who years later was to rope in an American boyfriend to help me in the 1945 general election. I never expected that! There was a big, tall blonde called Eileen, I remember, and then there was Evelyn and Rita, two fair-haired girls from Shepherds Bush who were to be with us, first on and off, and then permanently, for four or five years.

I led them into the field to try and instruct them. Not too easy to get them to take it seriously. Of course, the sugar beet was full of weeds and the first thing one had to do was deliver an elementary lecture on what a sugar beet looked like, and then how to chop them out in bunches at intervals. In some cases, when I looked back on their work, there were bunches of fat hen and sow thistle left standing proudly in position at proper intervals, with all the sugar beet removed, so I had to go over all the instructions again. After about an hour or so I had arranged for Will Barnet to come along and help and he, of course, was a bit better at teaching them than me. He laughed and joked with them, announcing loudly and clearly as he came into the field, 'I'll take the plump one!' And was met by some of the girls

with rather ribald jokes about tickling the roots of the plants.

By midday a certain amount of knowledge and a lot of exhaustion had set in. Some of the girls were flagging fast. I don't think this was quite what they expected on the farms; they had possibly expected to be helping jolly farmworkers in collecting hay, and so on, not doing this dull and repetitive work of chopping out unidentifiable plants. And later, somebody was going to have to get down and single the plants, disentangle the clumps . . .

During the course of the day, an upper-class lady from a few miles away, living in something-or-other manor, came around to see her 'gels'. She said she was responsible for their welfare and how were they behaving? They laughed fairly openly at her, I doubt they had met anybody quite like her before, and I don't think she could make much contribution to their welfare, although she probably did her best to make sure they got decent lodgings and things. I believe, though I don't exactly remember, that they started in some sort of hostel but were quickly farmed out in groups of two to lodgings.

Land girls were hired by the day from the War Ag., and when they were left on your farm, you had to employ them for that day, no matter what the weather did. If it rained you stood the loss of them standing around in the barns. Perhaps you would find them tidying up to do, but probably not, and their reaction, for the most part, if it was raining, was that you didn't work anyway. I remember the second day they started hoeing again, and then it poured with rain and they had to stop in a shelter. When it stopped raining the ground was too wet for hoeing and we took them out into the meadows with a varied assortment of bagging hooks and slashers to cut thistles. It wasn't profitable work — we could easily have done it with a horse mower — but it was something to keep them busy, and as regular farm people I think we thought it immoral for people not to be working.

On about the third day of sugar beet hoeing, I came to the conclusion that the one thing they were as good, or better, at than us was actually disentangling the plants. They were really rather hopeless at chopping with the hoe; half the time the blade of the hoe slipped over the top of the unwanted sugar beet plants and the weeds, leaving their roots intact. But the singling was a different matter: they didn't seem to mind getting on their hands and knees to do it — or at least they didn't express any disgust at the prospect — and their fingers were more nimble than ours.

And then we settled down to rather fewer land girls, four or sometimes six following behind us men, who were doing the chopping out, to do the singling. When the weather was nice I enjoyed it. I generally had working with me Evelyn Hawkins whom Albert Taylor dubbed the 'Boss's blonde'. She was an extremely attractive girl who told me a bit about her life in Shepherds Bush; her father worked on the underground, and she had rarely been out of London before. She and one of the other girls, Rita Bissell, had known each other all their lives, had been at school together and joined the Land Army together.

When eventually we got on top of the excess work we employed just the two girls, Evelyn and Rita, regularly. Lodgings were found for them quite nearby, first of all with a family in Chesham, and later with an old lady already in her seventies or eighties who lived only a short way away. They could then come to work on bicycles, which I think the authorities provided.

In different periods of my life, girls have seemed to concentrate on different aspects of their appearance; and perhaps it was being in some sort of uniform, perhaps it was the shortage of clothes in wartime, but Evelyn and Rita seemed to take enormous trouble with their hair. Evelyn's was dyed blonde, much blonder than it was naturally, and was always a mass of curls — her ideal must have been Betty Grable. The trouble Rita took was less obvious; both always looked very attractive, in my view.

From the word go, all the land girls seemed in my mind, consciously or unconsciously, to be absolutely obsessed with not going back to live in London. A few, a very few, made local boyfriends, but the vast majority seemed dead set on finding an American serviceman. Of those, by now, there were large numbers stationed at Bovingdon. Most of the station was out of bounds to all civilians, including the bomb dump which was next to our farm, but somehow they got in contact with each other. They went to dances that were held in Bovingdon and, according to Rita, who I have met again quite recently, the girls used to leave notes pinned to the trees on the edge of the bomb dump — notes addressed to American servicemen they had never even seen. The same obsession of getting out of England possessed quite a lot of local girls as well, so there was strong competition for the attention of the American servicemen. That occasionally led to trouble.

In my capacity as Home Guard, I quite often had to spend a Saturday night in the headquarters, a drill hall in Chesham where dances were held for the benefit of our comforts fund. Most Home Guards, being elderly, relied on two classes of people to support their dances, American servicemen and British servicemen, who in our case were based in Pipers Wood on the other side of Chesham. At one stage, I remember, a whole division of Scotsmen were there. The obvious preference of the local girls, including many of the land girls, for the Americans led to trouble. The Scotsmen tended to be quarrelsome anyway, and with this competition over the girls, it was hardly surprising that occasionally fights ensued. These fights worked very unfairly against the American servicemen because their own military police, known as 'snowdrops', who were large, boneheaded men with white helmets on, had a very simple instruction about how to deal with difficulty. They rendered their comrades insensible, threw them into the back of a lorry, took them back to Bovingdon and sorted them out. An over-simplification perhaps, but that's what it amounted to. On the other hand, the people who ran the Highland Division at Pipers Wood near Amersham, seemed to have been more relaxed and I never heard of any Scotsmen being so summarily dealt with.

None of this reduced the ardour of the land girls, who for the most part but not quite all, were keen to get out of Britain. Today one tends to forget how Americanized the 1930s in Britain were. Despite the Depression, the films of the time — nearly all American — depicted, for the most part, a glamorous lifestyle, with girls beautifully, if rather over-elaborately, dressed. And consciously or unconsciously millions of English girls believed that life in America was like that.

Quite predictably, Rita, who seemed the more sensible of our two girls, or at least the one with fewer glamorous dreams, finished up happily married in England, but Evelyn married a big, broad, American serviceman called Dale from the Bovingdon airbase. He was a sergeant on the ground staff, had innumerable stripes on his arm as they all had, and was a large, pleasant-looking man as I remember, though I never really talked to him. Some of the Americans didn't stand by their English girlfriends, but Dale Kinyon did and, duly, immediately after the war, Evelyn departed to go to America. I saw her twice after she had left the farm before she emigrated: once she came down and I took her to see some distant relations who happened to live nearby in Lee Common. The other time, I remember, I met her in Oxford Street, took her to lunch at Lyons Corner House and bought her a grey flannel suit to wear to America because she didn't seem to have anything suitable to wear for travel.

She left to go to Montana where Dale Kinyon's family were farmers. I don't know if she imagined that farming was anything like it is in Chesham, of course it wasn't. In that part of Montana it is very, very cold in the winter, pretty hot and dry in the summer and the wind blows. When she got to America, she wrote to us saying, 'Dale met me at the local station. He had glasses on and a stetson hat, and somehow he looked different.' Volumes couldn't have spoken more. The large and glamorous sergeant in uniform had become a farmer with glasses and a stetson hat.

We had letters every year at Christmas time and Florence always sent her a Christmas card. She seems to have got on all right, with several children, and we had pictures from time to time. She had become decidedly plump, and somehow looked very, very American, as did the whole set up. She had adapted to a place where you occasionally couldn't go out because the wind blew so much; where work was very hard and very seasonal; where the crops could fail completely, or be an absolute success. And she wrote knowledgeably about what they grew and how they grew it and about the market trends. She had adapted to a pioneering way of life.

And then, one Christmas, the letter didn't come and we didn't send another Christmas card because we didn't know why. Then after *Seventy Summers* came out, and Rita came to see me, she said that Evelyn had died a few years before. Apparently she had been home just once during all her marriage and hadn't stayed even for the time that she had arranged; she hadn't liked it in London, she had become completely American. I wish she had come to see me. I was glad that Rita had been; she gave me a photograph of Evelyn in her land army uniform. It was given with a kind smile.

In spite of her premature death, which, I understand, wasn't a prolonged one, hers was a relatively happy story: transported from one simple form of life in a small street in Shepherds Bush, with cinemas and entertainments within easy reach, to another simple form of life, out in the Montana countryside, with the wind blowing and the frost and the crops and the seasonal problems, and I think probably a close American family looking after her; at least I hope so. But that wasn't always the case. Other girls finished up in awful poor, white areas of the southern states of America, and I remember one from Ashley Green — a local girl, not a land girl — who smuggled out a letter to my mother for whom she had worked — literally smuggled it out because she was kept imprisoned by her husband — telling us of the terrible conditions she was living in, in some remote part of Louisiana. My mother arranged through American lawyers to go and get her out, and she was able to come home.

I don't know how many GI brides there are in America, and how many of their lives have been successes but, looking back, it is extraordinary how America became the Mecca for masses of them.

Those smiling, laughing girls arriving by lorry with their bright green jumpers, with their new, clean overalls wouldn't even recognize this place any more. The orchards where they used to scrump the fruit in summertime, with the high hedges where they used to skive out of the hot sun when we weren't looking. They're all gone, and the place is nearly an open prairie. Not, I imagine, like Montana, but maybe like some parts of America (and none the more attractive for that).

BADGERS

I have a special relationship with badgers. It might be described as a love-hate relationship. Before I knew anything about them, I loved them. Everything I had read made them out to be nice, clean animals that did nobody any harm. When I was young, there were not very many badgers in the Chilterns, and none whatsoever on our farm.

When I was about nine, a friend took me to watch a badger being dug out. There were some terriers tied up, and some implements of various sorts lying around including a dreadful-looking pair of tongs which were apparently to grab the badger out of his hole when they had dug down far enough, and two men digging. I thought the badger must have done something wrong — killed some chickens or something — so I asked one of the men, 'What's he done?' I remember very clearly that he replied, 'He ain't done nothing — he's just a badger.' It struck me as extremely unpleasant that somebody should be digging out a badger, for no good reason except that it was one. The friend who had taken me there obviously realized I was rather upset by it all, and probably did not like it much himself so he took me away and we never saw the badger.

Indeed, I did not see a badger for a great many years because, even if you have got them, you do not see them, as they move about in the night. Round about 1934 a family of badgers set up in a bank on our farm and they obviously prospered because, as the years went by, there were more and more holes in this bank and it became a city of badgers — a huge sett — and remains so to this day. All the time they did not do me any harm, and I still liked them.

Maybe ten years afterwards, we had a man working on the farm called Arthur, who lived in a bungalow at Bovingdon. This bungalow was a wooden building standing on pillars at the edge of a big chalkpit in which there was a badger sett. Arthur used to come in the morning moaning about these badgers, and I always used to say. 'They are good animals and do nobody any harm.' But he would say, 'Bugger the badgers — they wake my children in the night, grunting and snorting about under the house.' I told him how clean they were and how they dig their latrines away from their holes and keep the place clean around the holes. He said, 'I know they do — they dig them in my garden and that isn't very nice when you go digging potatoes and dig up one of their things.' I kept on thinking I was a friend of the badgers.

Two or three years after that, a neighbour rang up and said, 'You've got too many badgers on your farm — I'll come and get them out for you.' I said, 'No way, they are good animals. If they are not already protected, they ought to be and will be in a year or two.'

He said, 'Bugger the badgers. We went out to a chicken house and found dead chickens and a badger asleep on the job. He had killed the chickens and gone to sleep.' I consulted somebody about it and he said, 'Oh yes, just occasionally, a very old badger, who gets too idle to collect his natural food of grubs and things, will eat chickens but will almost always go to sleep on the job and get caught.' So I still thought this was not too bad. Poor old badger, after a long and blameless life, getting too feeble to go round all night to hunt for grubs, had the odd chicken and was killed. Still I defended the badgers, and still they kept multiplying and enlarging their sett, and soon they started appearing on other parts of the farm.

Then, in the middle 'fifties. I planted some fir trees quite near to their main sett and, in the second spring, the fir trees started disappearing. The mystery was solved months later when the badgers threw the bedding out of their sett to put in a clean lot and there, amongst the old bedding were the branches of my fir trees. They had apparently taken a liking to pine-scented bedding in their sett. Still, I defended them and thought on the whole they were good and harmless animals.

Many years afterwards in the 'seventies, we started growing maize for silage on the farm, by which time the badgers were everywhere. When the autumn came and the maize cobs were ready to be harvested, the badgers descended on the field every night like a herd of elephants, bashing down the maize plants and eating the cobs. I then began to think there were too many badgers.

As I walked through the maize on the day it was cut, I found one had actually started a sett in the middle of the maize field because he was too damned idle to come up from the main sett to eat the maize and just wanted somewhere to kip down when he had gorged himself. I thought they must be extraordinarily greedy or else there were an awful lot of badgers. Of course, because they had eaten so much, there were more of their latrines than usual and we had to walk very carefully in case we fell in one. Now, any time we grow maize anywhere, it is robbed by the badgers, bashed down by the badgers, and in the spring, after we've planted the following crop, they dig the land over trying to find the odd bits of maize cob that may have been left over and buried.

So I don't love badgers any more. As I walk around the farm, I smell them everywhere and I begin to hate them. When I read in the paper that they may spread TB to my pedigree cattle, I begin to wonder why on earth I protected them all those years ago when it would have been quite legal to eliminate them. From time to time I ring up the great world-famed expert on badgers, who lives not far away at Harpenden, and ask him what I can do to rid myself of the plague of badgers or, at least, reduce their numbers. Would he not like to dig some of them out and put them somewhere else where there aren't any badgers? But no help is offered. Everybody is a friend of the badger until they know them.

FLORENCE DIED IN
OCTOBER 1983

I used to lie on the hard, dry ground
And the grass sprang up around and cuddled me.
Sometimes, she lay down with me as well,
We laughed and cried and fought but, in the end, always loved.
And now I cannot lie down —
Not on the hard ground, with the grass to cuddle me.
If I did, I'd not get up again.
I am old.
The ground is too hard for me, and she is not there.
There is nobody to laugh with,
Nobody to cry with,
Nobody to fight with,
Nobody to fantasize with,
Nobody to just love like we used to.
The fantasies that never were have gone, or never could have been.
Oh, I can laugh still —
Laugh at jokes, but not with joy,
And I can cry still but cry alone.
Nobody to fight with — no fights that finish in love —
Just grass I cannot reach and ground that is too hard.
Why did we waste so much time,
Thinking about the state of a world we were too small to help?
Why did we not just lie on the ground and love,
While the grass was still long and warm?
Why did I go looking for other people
When I had already got what I still want?
I never really found them anyway.
Now I can walk in the grass, but I do not hear the songbirds any more
Or see their flapping wings.
They are still there a while
But,
In the end,
No small, twittering birds

No songs, whistles, no cooing doves —
Just murderous magpies,
And carrion birds calling their necrophiliac greed.
And then the grass all dead.

T.H.

NOVEMBER THE FIFTH

November 5th, 1987, was a perfect night for a bonfire. The flames shot straight up into the sky, dispersing whatever fog was in the immediate area, and we all sat around on bales as we have always done, while some members of the family let off fireworks in the background. As always, other people wandered in — nothing to do with us. One heard the odd voice in the darkness which you didn't know.

November 5th has always had a special significance for me. Perhaps it is because I was married on that date and all the way down to a miserable, wet Bournemouth where we spent our honeymoon, there were village bonfires set out ready. And if November 5th is one's wedding anniversary, one can hardly forget either event.

In times gone by there were always lots of hedge trimmings available at the beginning of November and it was easy to make a bonfire — with a big family you want a big bonfire. Nowadays the machines that have been brought into use chew up the hedge trimmings so that they don't require burning, you just plough them in. But always, as well as the hedge trimmings, November 5th was used as an occasion for clearing up the farm and burning whatever was left lying about which wasn't any good. Hemp bags with holes in them, paper, broken bits of wood and, I expect, old implements and things that would now be quite valuable.

I remember when in 1953 a tendency to clear up had rather a

disastrous consequence. Our fourth child had been born ten years previously and I don't expect anyone thought there would be any more, but my wife and I thought we were getting too old too quickly, so we would have another two, and on November 5th that year my wife went down to the bonfire, which was already alight and saw on top of it a dropside cot which she had been keeping and which had served the four children, a relatively new carrycot and several other items of that sort (old furniture used to get burnt as well). She didn't know what to do, she protested that they shouldn't have been put on there without her authority, and the farm chaps laughed and said, 'You won't be wanting that again!' She could hardly say, 'I've just been told that I'm pregnant again,' because it was only a matter of a week or two. And so, new cots and things like that had to be bought the following June.

The nature of the material of which bonfires are made has changed over the years; the hemp sacks with holes in have all gone, being replaced by plastic bags. They burn too; but with a nasty, acrid smell and lots of smoke. And we've got a new source of burnable material to replace the hedge trimmings — lots of things are delivered on pallets, wooden pallets, not all of which are returnable. And there always seems to be some shed which has been taken down somewhere, yielding very inflammable material, so we show no signs of running short, and if this annual clear-up round the farm didn't take place, we should be in a hell of a mess by now.

Each year since the war — they were too young before the war — the children and then the grandchildren have made a guy in the semblance of somebody they didn't care for. Because bonfires were banned during the war, Hitler wasn't burnt until 1945 when he was already dead. They burnt on occasion a couple of popes, or I believe perhaps the same pope twice; it wasn't anti-Catholic, teenage daughters just objected to something he had said. They wouldn't have dreamt of burning Pope John for instance, he was far too nice; but to show how ecumenical they all were, they also burnt an archbishop of Canterbury, several prime ministers, Enoch Powell, Mr Nixon, Stalin, all sorts of people, even poor Mr Heath, not so much because he was a villain but because it is so easy to make a guy in the semblance of Mr Heath. This year I asked the particular grand-daughter who had made the guy, who it was. She said, 'I don't really know. I made it like myself, I believe.'

That's a new departure. Perhaps they are running out of villains, Margaret has already been burnt once! Anyway, her guy was stuffed with paper and disappeared very quickly before I really had a chance to see it. As always we sat around on bales. We had to borrow these! We haven't got small bales anymore, only big round bales on which you can't sit. We sat around in a circle and watched the fire burn to sheer perfection, the best it's ever been, and in the background the older boys let off the fireworks, and in the darkness I heard strange voices that I didn't recognize — attracted by the fire to our field.

We used to cook potatoes and sausages in the hot ashes after the fire had burnt down. Now they bring them out ready-cooked, I don't know whether it is just the advance of modern technology within the family, or whether it is because the type of material the fire is built with nowadays wouldn't make them taste quite so good. Anyway, they taste much the same, and this year beetroot soup was added to the menu. But for me, all the time, it was a reminder that for forty-nine years it replaced wedding anniversary celebrations, and the memory of those bonfires on the way to Bournemouth on a drizzly November afternoon, all those years ago.

THE KILLERS

Our garden used to be full of songbirds, quite close to the house so that waking in the early morning was like waking in paradise. Under the eaves the swallows were nesting and every year in the stone wall there used to be a family of bluetits. This was somewhat harassing because they always had so many babies that over half of them fell out of the nest and died in spite of our efforts to return them, but some always survived.

From March onwards you could always hear a duck talking to her babies on the moat that went round the farm, and innumerable moorhens. Now it has all changed. If you listen hard, you can hear the dawn chorus of birds, but it is in the distance away from the garden and away from the farm. There are no swallows, and it is three or four years since I have seen a bluetit. The ducks arrive and nest and their young disappear. There are a few moorhens but nothing like the number there used to be.

I expect a lot of people living around here would say it was something to do with the farmers. We have removed the hedges in which the songbirds nested. We have poisoned the flies on which the bluetits fed. Something of that sort. It is bound to be the fault of the farmers, it always is. But in this case, it is nothing to do with my farming or anybody else's. There is still plenty of cover for the songbirds and, as far as I can see, plenty of insects for the tiny birds.

Most of the trouble dates from about nine years ago when our friends arrived to stay. It all started in the middle of the winter. One of the men on the farm came to me and said, 'There's a hawk owl in the cake house' (that's where you keep the cattle's food). I went and had a look, and sure enough a small brown owl was sitting on one of the bags of meal. It moved a little when I went in but didn't seem to be frightened.

For the remainder of that winter it flitted around the buildings, presumably feeding on vermin that lived in the cattle food, not doing anybody any harm, and nobody did it any harm. It was very small and everybody tells me that in little owls the male is smaller than the female, so it must have been a male. When the spring came he found himself a wife from somewhere and they settled down in an ivy-covered tree quite close to my house. They have been there ever since. I don't know whether it's the same couple or whether they handed over the tenancy to their last surviving children.

They seem to have an excellent family life. In the early summer one parent sits on a tree all day watching and guarding while the other one sits on the nest. When the young hatch out, they teach their family to fly right in front of us, and behave in a most responsible manner. Indeed, their route for teaching the young to fly is across my bedroom window and, in the early morning, the young will frequently perch on the sill. If they stay too long mother, or maybe father, will start screeching at them to come back, and if they do not come back, will fetch them just like a very well brought up family.

My wife used to love them particularly. She talked to them and they talked back to her. During the daytime, when you knew they were sitting around quietly somewhere but could not spot them, she would call to them and they would answer and then you could locate them.

Gradually, they appear to have wiped out almost all the other birds that used to live nearby. No more swallows come. The only survivors are a family of starlings, bang outside my window. They make a frightful noise in the early morning, squabbling about the food their parents bring home and crapping all down my window in a place which it is difficult for the window cleaner to get at. I expect that the little owls find them as repulsive as I do, and therefore do not eat their young or their eggs. Or else perhaps starlings have a collective security system and gang up to defeat marauding owls.

I simply do not know, but they have survived. Apparently, nothing much else has. Of course, it is not the little owls who take all the little ducks or ducks' eggs. That is the magpies or crows or foxes, which have multiplied.

Now the small birds in the immediate locality are so diminished that I have noticed the owl and the magpie quarrelling about territory. The owls seem to win; even in broad daylight I have seen them chase the magpies away. That in itself is a good thing because, although both are predators, the magpies and their methods are much more unpleasant than the owls. As a small boy I used to like them, with their smart black-and-white livery, hopping about in a self-confident way, until I realized they were disembowelling my chickens without even bothering to kill them. Then I turned against them.

Now, what do I do about all this? I could shoot the magpies if I had a gun, protected or not; but what about the owls, which are so attractive in their own ways and yet so destructive of other species? All the experts tell me that if you leave nature alone, it will find its balance. That may be so globally, but it is not so here where I want to enjoy it. And whether preserved or not, I cannot destroy the little owls. They were my wife's friends and they are my friends.

I cannot teach them to be vegetarians. The books tell me they eat lots of beetles. If they would continue to do that, they would have my blessing — who loves beetles? — but, at the moment, I cannot think of anything else except to bring back the gamekeepers and the revolting larders where they used to display their victims, bring back the death penalty for birds of prey. But I won't be the executioner.

CATS

About fifty to sixty years ago, there was a very rude poem circulating among schoolboys. The first four lines were 'Cats on the roof, cats on the tiles, syphilitic cats and cats with piles.' The remainder, I would not find it possible to repeat, even in these liberated days. It stuck in my mind because I have always felt it so accurately portrayed the fighting, hunting, quarrelling and free-love lifestyle of cats. It was obviously referring to cats in the town, but cats in the countryside, with half a chance, would behave in exactly the same way. In fact, I have often wondered if somebody actually composed it at the time or whether it was not simply a revised version passed down by word of mouth by boys since the Middle Ages, when people said what they meant, and when cats would be said to be suffering from somewhat different complaints. Possibly, now, there is a modern version circulating among schoolboys, with perhaps the cats having yet another set of diseases but the same pattern of behaviour.

Originally, in our farmhouse, there was a vast population of cats which lived in the kitchen, or rather slept all day in the kitchen. Some of them in various cupboards, some in a derelict baker's oven and some, generally the strongest and most assertive, under the big, black kitchen range. It was difficult to see how many there were, because we never saw them all at the same time. No doubt the population varied because, when they were about to give birth, they always remained outside and had their kittens in a safe place where nobody would find them to drown them. At nightfall, they were all let out and during the hours of darkness, some of them were hunting rats and mice around the farm, some of them patrolling the roofs in search of sparrows and sparrows' nests and yet others were out in the wood nearby catching small rabbits. If you observed them closely, they seemed to specialize. It was the same cats every time walking along the roof-line looking for sparrows' nests. They kept the farm largely free of all these pests before the days of rat-catchers, pest-control officers, rodent operatives, or the modern equivalent — who, in our case, calls himself 'The Pied Piper' — all with their buckets of poison, replacing the service the cats did in exchange for a purely nominal drink of milk when they returned to the farmhouse at dawn each day.

When my wife arrived on the scene, she did not like the idea of all these cats in the kitchen. They possibly were not all that clean so she decided they would have to live elsewhere and they were not allowed back in the house in the morning. They beat on our windows for days on end, for all the world like a revolutionary mob outside some royal palace. Indeed, in a sense, that is what they were because one is always being told that revolutions are caused by privileges withdrawn and not by longstanding injustices, and their privileges had been withdrawn. For several days, if the window was opened even a chink, a cat would place itself in the chink, spitting and cursing at us so that its mates could climb over its back and get into the house and disappear under the stove or into one of the cupboards. But, in the end, my wife, armed with a broom, won. The cats gave up the fight and either disappeared to other farms or lived permanently in the outbuildings and the woods. It may well be that many of the old cats were eaten by foxes, which, apparently, consider them a delicacy.

Now there is just one cat who lives in the farmhouse. Notwithstanding the fact that he is a tom, his name is Abigail, because, when he was very young, we made a mistake over his sex. He goes out every night and comes back every morning but he does not have such an adventurous life because the vet has destroyed all that. This sort of story is quite common among cats. When they are kittens, their owners think they are of one sex, take them for one sort of operation to the vet, then they have to have another sort. Your average suburban or town moggie, spoilt beyond belief, living its life on a cushion, using an earth-box for its natural functions because it cannot be allowed out, gets enormously fat and lazy, sleeping and dreaming all day of what its nature tells it it ought to be doing — hunting, feuding and making love outside. Many of them get their revenge on their owners by tripping up middle-aged ladies so that they break their legs and have to go to hospital or drop their crockery. Many a household tragedy of this sort is caused by a sleepy, over-fed and discontented cat.

On the other hand, even some highly domesticated cats are extremely intelligent. As teenagers my sister and I were taken on holiday to Cornwall, staying in a small bungalow at the top of the cliff. I remember it was called 'Windy Whistle', which was an appropriate name, since it was bitterly cold weather and the wind whistled around our bungalow all night. One night we returned home and found, waiting on the doorstep, a large, black-and-white cat — not your standard black cat with a white shirt front but one with black and white splodges and a little black spot under its chin so that it looked quite remarkably like the conductor, Thomas Beecham, with his evening dress and small black beard. The cat came in with us and from then on would not leave us for the remainder of the holiday. With or without the permission of its owners, if it had owners, it was decided we should take it home with us, some two hundred miles or more, to Buckinghamshire.

I remember it was an extremely hot day and the cat, after a while, would not sit quietly on our laps, so we had to drive with all the windows closed, especially as it did not appear to want to leave the county of Cornwall and, from the first few miles on, jumped for the window every time the slightest piece of it was opened. After a while, in the stifling heat, its hair started to come out and I am quite sure my mother would have wished to release the cat wherever we were at the time but could not face the scene that my sister would have undoubtedly made — and I should have been on her side.

Ultimately, we arrived home in Buckinghamshire and the cat was liberated. It promptly disappeared for forty-eight hours, exploring the area, no doubt, and finding its bearings. But it came back and carried out the normal cat existence — in the house during the daytime, out of the house at night — for some years afterwards. We called it Mawgan, after the place near where we had picked it up, because it was a Cornish cat. It was a quite remarkably intelligent animal. It used the lavatory in a proper, human manner. When they first saw it everybody was most intrigued to see it hop up on the seat and use the lavatory. Now a dog could not do that. A big poodle we have tried to get to use a children's pot, which was left lying about on the floor but he missed. Mawgan never missed because Mawgan was clever.

Cats do not want to be loved and to be dependent as dogs do, they want to be noticed and to be independent. If a cat knows somebody does not like them, they do not stay away, frightened, like a dog would, they rub against the person who does not like them to try to irritate them and be noticed. I understand that some people are allergic to cats and get asthma and, far from keeping away from them, cats brush up against them whenever possible, thereby making their presence felt in a big way — all ways of showing their independence. They do not mind in the least if people get irritated and try to kick them because it is almost impossible to successfully kick a cat. It is always quicker than you are. Abigail sits on my favourite seat but nobody has ever yet succeeded in sitting on him. He is far too quick.

FOXES ARE SURVIVORS

Foxes are winners; foxes are survivors. I have a feeling that, if mankind laid waste the world and destroyed himself, the foxes would still be there, feeding on the rats that would also survive.

They do not just feed on chickens. They will eat almost anything, alive or dead; the contents of your dustbin just as willingly as your chickens or your pet cat or rats that live around the place. They will eat grain and, according to Aesop's Fables, grapes. They can run as fast as most dogs. They are so much cleverer than dogs that it takes thirty dogs guided by several men to catch them. They can climb trees just as well as a cat and can swim, which a cat can only do with difficulty. They can live above the ground, they can live on roofs, or they can live in holes in the ground.

I do not think they particularly like the work of digging holes — they would rather make use of what the badgers, who are really dedicated diggers, have done or what the rabbits, also good diggers, have done. Foxes generally take possession of other animals' holes and enlarge them to use as their own homes.

Foxes have been at war with men for a very long time. When I first remember, the war was more or less static. The countryside was controlled by landowners, who employed people to make sure that the foxes survived in the off season so that they could be hunted in the hunting season. The same landowners employed game-keepers to preserve their pheasants. Unknown to their employers, the gamekeepers attempted to poison the foxes with strychnine and other killers. I do not think they were very successful and the foxes still survived.

In those days, say 1920, foxhunting was done by the landed gentry and larger farmers: the ladies, looking rather glamorous, riding side-saddle, in beautifully cut habits, top hats and veils, the men looking somewhat boozed and bloated. Later on, the women started riding astride like men, took off their veils, and you saw that they were also somewhat bloated.

I was always a bit against hunting, not especially because of the cruelty it involved because there was so much worse cruelty going on, but principally because the people who did it were so damned arrogant. When I first started farmwork it appeared that, because I was working and they were on a horse, they expected me to acknowledge them and pull my forelock like some peasant. Indeed, I felt rather like a medieval peasant with a lot of knights and barons on horses riding over the land I was trying to cultivate, damaging the crops. If I had had a pike in my hand, I would have felt like sticking it up their bracket. I imagine this was the way a medieval peasant must have felt.

Gradually, the landowners, through taxation or incompetence, abandoned their land, at least in our district. They either went to live in London, if they had sufficient income, or emigrated to places like Kenya where there were 'more staff available, my dear'. The hunting was then taken over by business people and so it survived until the war.

When the war was over and it all started up again, our hunt had a new master — a Mr Barratt, the man who made the liquorice allsorts. A hunting farmer neighbour, notwithstanding my known hostility to hunting people, came round to introduce Mr Barratt to me. At that time I was waging war against foxes because I had free-range chickens and the foxes had been attacking them. They appeared to do it mostly for fun, not for food. Do not let animal lovers tell you foxes only kill chickens to eat; they kill a dozen and eat one because they enjoy the job. I have seen them do it.

Anyway, the hunting farmer introduced me to Mr Barratt and Mr Barratt said he hoped I would be co-operative. I pointed out to him that, at that moment, I was conducting my own private war against the foxes with use of gelignite anti-tank grenades, which were left over from my service in the Home Guard during the war, which I should not have had. (I hope after all these years nobody can prosecute me for it.) I described to the Master of the Hunt how I put these 3½ lb grenades down the foxes' earths, wired them up, and blew them up electrically, and how humane I thought it was. Mr Barratt laughed and the hunting farmer looked absolutely aghast.

We had previously had in the family a wild fox which we had tamed. His name was Freddie and he was a most attractive character. He was really fond of human beings. If you lay down in his pen, he would come and play in your hair. He would comb through your hair, I suppose looking for parasites, and was obviously quite fascinated by it. He would never attempt to bite. When he got out, the method of catching him was to lie down and he could not resist coming to play in your hair, and you would then try to grab him.

But one day he got out into some free-range chickens, some white leghorn pullets with which I was very pleased. White leghorns are a very active breed of poultry (they probably barely exist nowadays). They are light, quick and active but, before my very eyes, Freddie had had the heads off half a dozen of them and was literally laughing over his shoulder at me while he did it. Then he seized just one of them and ran off into the wood. This is what makes me think that foxes take chickens as much for fun as for food. Of course I was furious. I do not carry a gun and so I could not shoot him. The problem arose as to how to catch Freddie.

A friendly local doctor gave us some chloroform and we placed this on one of the dead hens and trailed it around the wood where Freddie was known to be. After a long, long time, he came out, smelt it, smelt it again, got a bit dozy, and we grabbed him. He lived for some years afterwards in a pen. A wife named Vicky was acquired for him but they never bred. They were wonderfully attractive pets, apart from the awful unearthly noises and the ghastly smells in the mating seasons. But no cubs ever arrived.

In the post-war period, when the hunt had become entirely dominated by business people, Mr Barratt's job was taken over by a very successful pork butcher, a nice man who bought pigs from us and apologized when his hounds over-ran our pig runs. Still I was hostile to them, but not in a very active way. Then one day, two of our children came in crying and saying a fox had just jumped into our moat with a lot of dogs after it, and it was frightened to death.

Sure enough, we looked into the garden and the place was full of men on horses and hounds. My wife rushed to the door and, from her full five foot one inch, addressed the master of the foxhounds, the successful pork butcher: 'Get your bloody dogs out of this garden at once.' I could see his mouth framing the words, 'Hounds madam' but seeing her determination, all the self-confidence which being on a horse and which his perfectly cut red coat and his top hat gave him, evaporated. He turned tail like a small boy and got his men to call hounds and horses out of our garden and out of our yard. I went into the garden and a bedraggled-looking fox was sitting on the other bank of our moat, shivering or shaking, or was it shaking with laughter?

Now, the sweet manufacturers and the pork butchers have been taken over by multinationals and no longer do they go out hunting. The control of the local pack in a semi-suburban area has returned to farmers. The people who run the multinationals are too busy fending off take-over bids to spend time hunting. I think perhaps their wives hunt and certainly some of their daughters do. In fact, apart from a few farmers, it has become a woman's occupation. Even some of my own family have started to hunt, so I cannot any longer feel quite so hostile to it as there are much worse things going on in the world.

Meanwhile, my own private war with the foxes is over. You cannot keep chickens outside any more. You cannot keep free-range chickens because people who have developed systems of keeping chickens in cages have made it uneconomical to allow chickens to go free. Huge companies now produce chickens on a large scale and they have destroyed the farmyard fowl and deprived the foxes of their fun but not of their diet. Myxomatosis has killed off the rabbits which the foxes used to eat, but that does not bother them either. They have turned their attention more and more to towns, to living on the contents of people's dustbins, and to killing rats, of which they are very fond. According to the BBC they live on the roofs of town houses as well as in holes in my wood. I do not doubt it for a minute.

For some reason or other, I still allow people to shoot some of them at harvest time in the cornfields, but it is time I stopped because now I think they are far more effective in dealing with rats and mice than any company that specialises in pest destruction. Everywhere I go on the farm, I see where the foxes have dug rats out of holes. They have plenty of time. They enjoy their work, and they enjoy eating rats. I have nothing against them.

Now, our neighbouring farmer comes round before they go hunting, he tells me where they are going, he puts up fences at suitable places for them to jump, he repairs the fences if they break them, he thanks me, and it is altogether a great deal more civilised than it used to be. My family assure me they never catch any foxes — or practically never.

At the moment, the foxes are easily winning the war because fewer hands are turned against them, fewer game-keepers are about, fewer farmers are protecting their free-range hens. So there are more foxes. The sheer number of foxes makes the job of the hunt more difficult because, no sooner do the hounds get the scent of one fox than they cross the track of another, so frequently get diverted. Perhaps the foxes have worked out a relay system to tire the hounds out?

SOMEBODY WANTS TO KILL!

On August 12th each year the grouse season starts. Grouse shooting is the peak of the competitive slaughter industry. Generally, the so-called quality papers and magazines, like *Field* and *Country Life*, which most of us only see in the dentists' or doctors' waiting rooms, show pictures of the occasion and of superior people, distinguished people, titled people, royal people, dressed in unusual clothes, standing in some bleak moorland scenery, carrying guns. Maybe, in the distance, you can just see some hardy Highlanders walking the hillside, driving birds towards the people with guns so that they can shoot them — small birds, which when they are cooked, taste as if they had lived all their lives on tarmac that has given them a distinctly tarry flavour. These small birds have been carefully protected from their enemies for the remainder of the year.

Simultaneously, dishonest restaurateurs and wholesale butchers are rushing to the restaurants the same type of little bird, which they have had in cold storage since last year, so that they will have it on their menu before anybody else, allegedly just shot and at a huge price. Later on, in other parts of the country, partridges — somewhat similar small birds but tasting much nicer — are treated in the same manner but never with the same social prestige attached to either the shooting or the eating of them.

Then, of course, on a huge scale there are pheasants, more beautiful and bigger than the other species, but totally domesticated and tame, almost all reared carefully by gamekeepers in order to be released and driven in the air to be shot. Many of them start their life being hatched out and mothered by an ordinary domestic hen and are forced to go wild later on. This is a real killing business — a real, big killing business. At the very best shoots, many, many hundreds of these tame birds are shot. This has been going on a long time. King Edward VII, apparently, fancied himself at this type of slaughter. When it comes to killing, how much difference is there between driving pheasants, which have been carefully protected and reared, over the top to men with guns, carefully positioned in order to be able to shoot them — how much difference between that and walking into a shed full of chickens, catching them and wringing their necks?

As for me, I am not a competitive killer by nature. Shooting pheasants in competition with other men, proving I am better at it than they are, means absolutely nothing to me, any more than I have ever had any ambition to work in a slaughterhouse. Even sitting on a chilly river bank, fishing to catch bigger fish than anybody else, does not thrill me in any way. In fact, for me, the fish is the most unfortunate of the lot. I think he is entitled to as much consideration as anybody else and to see him gasping for breath in an alien element has always worried me, especially when I know he has a damned great gash in the roof of his mouth.

Some of the nicest people I know, and the kindest people I know, enjoy shooting pheasants and landing fish, and I enjoy eating both of these things, and I persuade other people to come on my farm to shoot the pigeons which are eating our crops, to say nothing of gassing the rabbits and poisoning the rats. So perhaps the people who actually do the job are closer to man's real nature than me, because man is designed as a predator. His place in the world is founded on him being a predator, and predators maintain the balance in nature, most of them by accident — whereas man can do it by design.

The trouble with man is that he has always been too successful and can so easily wipe out other species. The only protection other species have against him is man's conscience. He is different from the other predators, as he apprehends what may happen and has a feeling of responsibility for it after it has happened. In the past, man has deliberately destroyed other predators, has reduced the hawks, the owls, foxes, weasels, stoats and polecats, in order to preserve both his domestic animals and poultry and also his beloved game birds, which he wants to kill himself. By destroying these predators, he has often upset the balance of nature. Maybe if he ceased trying to be a predator himself, he would upset it just as much. Because we have a sense of guilt for what we have done, we have imposed on ourselves a duty to preserve all the other species from ourselves, and to some extent from each other, in an attempt to maintain a balance of nature, partly as it originally was or, more largely, as is appropriate for the way we have altered the world.

Meanwhile, the local urban population practically queues up to ask me for the right to shoot pigeons on our crops and to ferret rabbits out of holes in our hedges. If I advertised to let the right to shoot what few wild pheasants and partridges there may be on the farm, I would have a lot of takers.

A lot of people seem to want to kill. I am a bit of a freak — I only want to eat what other people have killed. Those who want to do the killing are in other ways no more brutal than anybody else. In fact, they seem to be a majority of the population, and I am co-operating in the business and encouraging them to do it on my farm. I am eating the dead birds. So why do I find the picture of King Edward VII, surrounded by vast rows of dead pheasants which had been carefully reared, absolutely revolting — worse than a conveyor belt of turkeys in Mr Matthew's slaughterhouse?

THE NIGHT THE PIGS ALL DIED*

Over five thousand of them sat down that night to a vegetarian meal in the new, huge, vegetarian restaurant just off the Great West Road. They had a meal of nuts, beans and salads from all over the world, with plenty of alcohol, because that is all vegetable. The walls were adorned with gory pictures of slaughterhouses and things that would never happen again. The catering firm had built the restaurant many years before to protect themselves against the possibility of what later was to happen. They made the decision to go vegetarian after all the food on their refreshment counters in Earls Court had been poisoned during Smithfield Show week, and the show had to be abandoned. They suffered their losses and prepared for the future.

The gentle people's campaign had been long and hard. Many of them at first had suffered quite considerably until they got the ascendancy over everybody else. Long before debate took place in Parliament, people had been worn down by small pressure groups

*The publisher and Ruth Boyd would like to dissociate themselves from this piece.

everywhere shouting obscenities when they were eating in restaurants, demonstrating outside slaughterhouses, poisoning food and, sometimes, even blowing up the slaughterhouses. In the end, people just could not be bothered. If the protesters wanted it to happen so badly, let it happen.

The majority of the Members of Parliament were not convinced. Some had always been supporters of reform. Most of them just gave way to the energetic pressure groups who thought that solidarity with animals was the most important issue that had ever been and that many must not kill and eat any animal ever. A few older members in the Commons, and even more in the Lords, tried to stem the pressure and pointed out some of the dangers. Man originally, in the stone-age days, had been mainly carnivorous. He had lived by hunting, also collecting nuts and berries, but primarily by hunting and fishing.

But the reformers would not have this. They just would not believe it. People who lived in peace and tranquillity in an idyllic world could not possibly have brought themselves to kill anything. It could not be true. Remember Piltdown Man. Scientists have often faked history. When somebody tried to reason with them, he would be shouted down with continuous cries of 'Nuts, nuts, nuts . . .' or occasionally, christened the Piltdown Man.

Some religious groups had tried to fuel opposition. Jewish organisations declared that kosher slaughtering and the eating of meat were part of the Jewish tradition and that kosher slaughtering was absolutely humane and should be exempt from any regulations. The Muslim community, by now very strong, said that from the beginning Mohammed had accepted the eating of meat, so it was right for them, and their particular method of slaughter was right for animals. But nobody would hear any of it. The Hindu population, also by now quite considerable, had no strong views about it. Indeed, they were better prepared by their traditions to deal with the situation than anybody else.

So the Act was passed and, as from April 1st, no butchers shops were to be opened, no slaughterhouses were to operate, no animals were to be slaughtered for human consumption, and restaurants that served meat would be prosecuted. The advocates of the Bill said there was provision for everything. There would be re-training courses for the younger butchers and slaughtermen in hydroponics so that they would not lose anything by the change; the older ones could live on their pensions. Of course, livestock farmers had no right to any compensation. After all, they have been profiteering out of the rest of the population for thousands of years. When somebody said they had always lived at a lower level than the urban population, they were not believed. It was just supposed to be special pleading.

In the days before April 1st, there was frantic slaughtering. People who were strongly addicted to meat ate nothing else. The dog-food firms filled every tin that they could find and wondered what they would do when they had sold them all. In the meantime, they would, no doubt, do very well. A commission of vets and food manufacturers sought to find viable substitutes for dogs. There were problems because protein seeds and vegetables throughout the world were going to be in short supply. The Scottish Nationalists were complaining bitterly that the Department of Agriculture for Scotland had neglected its duty in the preparatory period by not breeding some form of bean or nut which would grow in the Outer Hebrides. What were people going to do without sheep there? They could not eat the sheep — they could keep them for the wool, but they could not eat them.

As the gentle people all sat down to their vegetarian dinner, the slaughtermen were engaged in a last frantic effort to destroy all the pigs in the country, all the turkeys in the country, and a great part of the sheep and all the beef cattle. It had been considered advisable to place small numbers of all the species in various zoos up and down the country so that the population could go and see specimens of the poor creatures on which their ancestors had battened, but all the rest had to go.

Of course, nobody in the industry could conceive it was ever really going to happen, so the last minute rush was terrible. They could not hear it in that catering firm's air-conditioned dining room, but there was more squealing going on in the slaughterhouses of Britain that night than ever. Pigs were being killed as fast as men could handle them and men were working like demons, knowing that they would never have to do it again. Out in the countryside, all the knackers had been pressed into service. Farmers were digging pits, destroying their animals and putting them in the pits because there was no market for them.

The celebration was going well at the vegetarian dinner. Nobody would ever soil themselves by eating meat again. Animals were their brothers and it was tantamount to cannibalism to eat them. During the evening, somebody asked the chairman, 'What shall we do now that the campaign is over — there's nothing to campaign about?' He said, 'Oh, we have missed a few things along the way. Oysters are such simple creatures that they were not covered by the Bill and, no doubt, greedy people will be gorging themselves on poor oysters from now on. So we will have to bring in another Bill to stop their slaughter. You'll remember we brought in the fish-with-gills during the course of the Bill through Parliament.' And they all looked forward to another campaign.

A week or two later, it became apparent that in the Third World, people were suffering from a total lack of protein because their governments and their businessmen, anticipating the demand, had sold all the high protein seeds — all the beans, all the peas, all the nuts — to Britain and had made a killing, that is, in financial terms, and their own people were getting desperately short. Recriminations started and everybody blamed everybody else for not making proper plans.

Of course, people were still getting milk. But milk prices rocketed. It soon became apparent that if you had to throw cows away when they were old, and throw all the males away anyway, milk cost a lot more to produce. Well, that is an easy one to answer: dairy products are bad for you anyway. That has been known for a long time. Woollen clothing began to get as dear as fur coats had been years ago before they were abolished. Of course, fur coats were the first thing to go. But now, you could not eat the sheep so you could not keep as many, so the wool was in very short supply and very expensive.

The gentle people, the animal lovers, had done their work. In Britain at least, nobody was killing and eating poor animals. Some were eating meat on their holidays but, soon, a test would be devised so that meat eaters could be detected when they returned to Britain and treated. No squealing pigs were being loaded into lorries to go to slaughterhouses, Indeed, there was no squealing because there were no pigs and the campaigners glowed with self-righteousness. But they had not found a way to prepare food for the dogs from vegetables and the dogs had not been reformed and still killed rabbits and rats. So, kill the dogs — kill all the dogs.

After a while, the children threw away all their toy farm animals because they did not know what they were, and demanded more rockets.

BEWARE OF THE COW

Bulls have always had a very bad press. They seem to be symbolic of strength and aggression and male chauvinism in its worst form. Cows are always pictured as being docile, friendly creatures who never hurt a fly. This is not the whole truth. Whereas it is perfectly true that bulls are extremely strong and very clumsy, so you do not want to get in their way, they are not all that much more dangerous than cows under certain circumstances.

Most of the people who are injured by bulls, and sometimes killed, are in fact stockmen looking after them, who get in their way or who get over-confident in handling them. The general public, out rambling or whatever, does not confront them or get in their way, and is most unlikely to be involved in any trouble, whereas if they go near a cow which has recently calved, especially if they are leading a dog or with a loose dog, then there is likely to be trouble. Like most people who have worked a long time with cattle, I have been bashed up by cows but never by a bull, even though one has had to handle them under difficult circumstances.

Cattle themselves seem less conscious of differences in sex than any animal one can think of. I have a clear memory of when I was about eighteen, of my stepfather, who is a townsman, rushing in and saying to my mother, 'Jean, Jean, I've seen a lesbian cow'. The fact is that if there is not a bull in the field, the cows will try to do for their friends what he would do. Most of the management of dairy herds where there are no bulls running depend on this propensity. They see a cow behaving like a bull and they know that the one she is jumping on needs the bull, so they call the artificial insemination man. The dairy industry would half collapse without that tendency. So do not assume that what acts like a bull is a bull. Likewise, bulls do not seem all that conscious of sex either. They will light-heartedly attempt to mate with males and females regardless.

When I was young, we had a herd of Ayrshire cattle which were extremely active. They had long horns which, in those days, we did not take off, under the mistaken impression that they could do no more damage with the horns than they could do without them and, in any case, the horns were handy to lassoo them with if you had to catch them under difficult circumstances. At the time I had a girlfriend whose stepfather was a colonel in the regular army, and had a small herd of Guernseys as a hobby. One day my Ayrshire bull got out with his Guernseys and I had an irate telephone call.

I had no alternative but to do what one should not do, confront the bull and remove him back to my own premises. Now I knew that, before he came towards you, he would always try to get a suitable run — he would step back a pace or two to get a run at you. Therefore, I knew my only hope was to get a pitchfork, which he would not face, and back him the two hundred or so yards home. I did this in fear and trembling all the while with complete success, and was astonished to hear the colonel telling his friends a few days later, 'This young man confronted the bull and forced it back just by fixing it with his eye.' Nothing could have been farther from the truth.

The same bull, who was a very active animal, got out in the middle of the night and another neighbour phoned me up: 'Your bull is blowing under my front door.' As it was pitch dark, this was a frightening prospect. I went out with a young lad, each of us with a torch, and we decided that if we turned a torch on, the bull would come towards us; so we relayed him all the way home which, in this case, was about half a mile, getting about a hundred yards ahead, turning the torch on so he came towards it, while the other went nearer home, and so on. We led him all the way home. But when we got him back into his own shed and turned the electric light on, his eyes were pouring with tears. He had been frightened to death by the whole experience.

In later years we have had cattle grazing in a park near to a town. There was considerable trouble because people kept breaking the fences down and the cattle kept getting out and either getting into people's gardens or eating the poisonous yew trees on nearby property. The stockman had the brilliant idea of putting a ring in a cow's nose. This, he reckoned, would keep people away. Within two days I had a telephone call from the local police: 'You've got a bull in the park — it's illegal.' It was then. 'I shall have to report you, but you had better get it out of the park.' I said, 'I'm sorry but we have no bull in the park.' He said, 'I've seen it myself — I saw the ring in its nose.' I had to say, 'You'd better go and look at the other end.'

He rang off and I heard no more, but the fences required much less repairing for the next few weeks. That particular cow was well chosen for the job because she was very friendly and when anybody came in the park, she came forward to talk to them. But she was quite safe.

I have myself been bashed black and blue by an elderly cow, imagining that she was protecting her newborn calf, because I misguidedly went into the field with a dog. Cows hate dogs, so the general public should not take them into fields where there are cattle.

Lately, I have detected a more sensible attitude from the public towards cattle. Even the Ramblers' Association — sworn enemy of bulls — has had the grace to refer to dangerous animals rather than just bulls, which I find an improvement. And, in the same park I mentioned, when I went over one Sunday morning to see how our bull was working — it now being legal to have him there — I saw from a distance that he was attempting to do the work for which I keep him.

There was a line of people watching him, a tall, bearded man, a lady with large spectacles and a long dress, and three children — the sort of family who, in the past, you looked upon as *New statesman* readers, or perhaps *Guardian* readers. He was lecturing his family on the facts of life in the most lucid and clear manner, using my bull as a practical demonstration. He appeared to be unafraid of him. He was not interfering with his job and he had no reason to be afraid.

If you are on a footpath, keep away from the bulls but, even more so, keep away from small calves. If the cows are black and white, they probably have not got a bull with them anyway — he is probably tied up in a shed or he probably comes from the AI station by proxy. If they are Jerseys, distinguished by their pretty, gentle faces, hopefully there will not be a bull there because, if there is, he will be very nasty; but almost certainly he is chained up in the farm. If they are beef cattle with calves at foot and they are black with no horns, keep out of the way of the cows. They are much worse than the bulls.

If they are tall and muscular and fawn and you are not in the county of Devon, where they will be very placid south Devons, they will be imported Limousins from France, and most likely if you clap your hands, they will all disappear over the nearest hedge because they are terribly nervous — only dangerous if you happen to be picnicking on the other side of the hedge. If they are large and white, they are Charolais. The bulls are quite quiet but, again, keep away from the cows if they have small calves.

Never take dogs in the field. Dogs are more dangerous than bulls anyway. For myself, I am frightened to death of horses.

THE SUFFOLK STALLION

It all started with Meg, a fat, black Shetland pony, when I was about nine years old. My sister, who was older than me, got on Meg quite a lot. As far as I can remember, I only got on once and then I fell off, hitting my head on a lump of concrete. It knocked me literally silly. It appears that I rushed into the house, through the kitchen, picked up a plate of egg sandwiches, which had been prepared for a number of people to eat, and shut myself in the lavatory with them. I think I had the vague idea that I was somewhere safe, for the rest of my life on a diet of egg sandwiches of which I was particularly fond. Anyway, I would not come out and they fetched the doctor, an amusing Irishman called Dr Heron, who rode a motorcycle, and he, through the lavatory door, persuaded me out. He had a look into my eyes, and said, 'The boy's got concussion,' and I was put into a dark room for the night. By the morning I was more or less all right, but not prepared to try Meg again.

My sister and I used to be allowed to lead the horses back from the field to the farm, during harvest, and lead the empty carts out again. This was all right; farm horses move so slowly that you couldn't get into any difficulties, except that they occasionally trod on your toes with their big, flat feet. Or even hit the gateposts because you guided them wrong, but going so slowly that no damage was ever done. About this time my sister and I planned to write a book about farm animals. She insisted on writing the first chapter which was to be about Shetland ponies. In vain, I argued that Shetland ponies were not farm animals; she argued that they were in the Shetlands. But worse was to come, she started her chapter with what, to me, were extremely embarrassing words: 'These lovely little animals . . .' I couldn't stand it; they weren't lovely. I gave up the idea of writing a book with her, I don't know how far she got with it.

I started, at an early age, reading *The Farmer and Stockbreeder* and cutting out pictures from it of the various types of animals. I was particularly taken with Suffolk horses; to me they looked much more practical for our type of land than the shires. They had less hair on their feet which, in the case of shires, got very dirty and they contracted the most unpleasant disease called 'greasy heel' which

smelt and looked awful. And so I started to discuss them with George Larkin who then managed the farm. There was on the farm a shire mare called Dolly and every year they bred a foal from her, always using the shire stallion that travelled the area in the spring, visiting farm after farm with groom in charge. I tried to persuade George Larkin that it would be much better to use a Suffolk stallion. He didn't argue with me much, which is amazing since it was April 1926 and I was just fourteen years old.

One afternoon he said, 'Come across tomorrow morning at eight o'clock, and you can take Dolly over to Watford where there's a Suffolk stallion.' I hadn't really bargained for that, but I could hardly back out. I'd never been by road to Watford, and didn't know the way. However, I got lots of instructions and at eight o'clock the next morning somebody hoisted me up onto Dolly's broad back and we ambled off, to Watford. There was little or no traffic then on the lane, which was still largely gravelled, not tarmac, and about three-quarters of a mile away from the farm I went onto a green lane, now the main road to Bovingdon but then just a wide, green stretch; and I went, I suppose, nearly a mile along it to a point called Pudd's Cross. I'd been there before and it was like a frontier post to me, it was on the boundary between Buckinghamshire and Hertfordshire, it said so. There the green lane crossed a main road. I had plenty of time to think on Dolly, she went so slowly, and I thought to myself; Pudd's Cross? Is this where the vast amount of Puddephatts who now inhabit Buckinghamshire crossed from Hertfordshire? And I imagined them, like the Israelites of old, crossing over; no waters to part, although if you did it today, the traffic on that main road would be just about as difficult as the waters of the Red Sea.

From then on, I was in unfamiliar territory, places I'd only heard of, not seen: Belsize, Hog Pits Bottom, Sarratt, signposts to Flaunden and Chipperfield. It was April and the bottoms of the hedges were beginning to green, the blackthorn well in flower, and some fruit trees. It was a mild day, and peaceful enough, but riding Dolly was painful, she was so wide my legs were nearly split, I wasn't all that big then. Eventually, through all this unfamiliar territory, feeling like some sort of an explorer, I came to a long lane which had been described to me as going down to the edge of Watford; I didn't have to go through the town. I arrived at half past twelve. It had taken four and a half hours to travel, I suppose, eleven or twelve miles.

There was a big stable with loose boxes, and a pair of farm cottages. I knocked, as I'd been told, on the door of the first one and a rather grumpy, tall, angular man called out to me, through a mouthful of food, 'I'll come out when I've had my dinner,' and a fat slovenly woman looked approvingly at him, she didn't want his meal disturbed. So I tied Dolly to a fence and waited apprehensively. Apprehensively because an enormous ginger head popped out over one of the stable doors — it was the Suffolk stallion. He proceeded to beat on the doors with his front hooves, which caused sparks to fly, as the door was clad with steel. He seemed to be blowing fire and brimstone from his nostrils, and snorting, and the heads of Suffolk mares popped out of the other boxes and looked on expectantly, waiting I suppose for their lord and master to spring into action. I waited there one whole hour and the grumpy man came out, and with no sign of enthusiasm, or nervousness, put a halter on the enormous head, opened the door and led out the Suffolk stallion. The horse immediately stopped banging and snorting and walked gently up to the back of Dolly, and did absolutely nothing.

With that the groom started to curse and swear: 'You idle fat bugger, never did like work, did you? For God's sake, get on with it.' And the Suffolk mares from their boxes whinnied encouragingly — at least I supposed so. In the end, quite suddenly, he did what he was required to do and was immediately led back into his box, sweating profusely and no longer looking so powerful or self-confident. I gave the man the money that I'd been given for him.

Dolly and I then ambled back home, by this time my legs aching almost unbearably. I contemplated trying to sit sideways, as the farm man often did on the horse. I realized that if I slipped off, there was no possibility of getting on again, and I would have to walk home; so I bore the pain in my legs and we ambled back, the countryside by this time not looking as interesting as it had in the morning.

We finally got back, after my normal teatime. Dolly did not conceive and I always had a feeling that the farm people blamed me and that in some mysterious way it was my fault. Dolly should have been mated to her own kind of shire, and anyway the shire stallion visited, you didn't have to go and visit him. So we had no Suffolk horses on the farm, nor Suffolk crosses either, for more than twenty years, when I bought two or three for myself. I was by then farming independently. They were a success; extremely docile and hard working, but of course they were overtaken very soon by the tractors which blew sparks and snorted like that stallion long ago had done. Regrettably, the Suffolks were sold, some at least of them probably ending up being eaten in Belgium. It was a mistake; if I'd kept them and bred a few, by now they would have been worth a bomb if exported to America for use as pets.

I'D GIVE MY HEART
TO A PIG!

All the publicity about the possibility of using pigs' organs to transplant into human beings, seems to have shocked a lot of people. Not me. Pigs' organs are likely to be the same as ours. A pig's diet is largely cereal, supplemented by both animal and vegetable protein — that's what we need and that's what they need — so naturally our organs will be much the same.

As a surgeon put it, pigs are horizontal men and men are vertical pigs. It's pretty well what George Orwell said all those years ago; his pig, once he started dominating the farm, got up on his hind legs and walked around like a man.

A few years ago, when they were hostile to the police, young people referred to them as pigs. I've often thought that if pigs communicate with each other no doubt they use the term 'man' as one of opprobrium, after the way we treat them.

I've always been keen on the idea that something of mine might be of use to another human being when I am dead — I still am, but I think I'm too old, mostly worn out. My heart and liver are showing signs of wear and tear and no surgeon would want to use them. I don't know about my kidneys. My eyes cannot see to read, although they can see to get me about.

The idea I have now is that I will leave my body to some experimental institution who might use my organs to transplant into an elderly sow, to give her perhaps the chance of an extended family life, or a happy retirement on an experimental farm — I wouldn't like her to be slaughtered with part of me in her. If she'd gone blind, my poor old eyes would enable her to get about, and she wouldn't want to read anyway. And maybe those other organs of mine would be enough for the normal expectation of life of a pig. Anyway, I would like the idea of a happy old sow with a bit of me in her, having a slightly extended life.

If the idea were taken up, I expect some people would be shocked and horrified, especially those who are always so busy looking after other people's ethics. But perhaps it is good for people to be shocked. I think it helps to make them think, and well-intentioned people often don't think through their ideas to a logical conclusion.

For me, the most successful thing I've done, in my short and unimpressive career as a journalist, was an article that stated, amongst other things, that if the animal rights people had their way and the slaughter of animals for human consumption was stopped, all the pigs in the country would die at once. That is undeniably true; they would not be kept. I had no idea, until then, what vast supplies of vitriol mild and kindly people have in their bloodstream ready to pour out on the head of people who shock them, and it was then that I discovered that 'Disgusted of Tunbridge Wells' really does exist. He wrote saying I must be very ignorant; pigs would still be kept to make dung for him to use on his allotment.

Meanwhile, if my experiment was put into effect, maybe it would sink into the minds of just one or two people that whatever is unique about man, whatever differentiates him from other animals — his spirit, his soul, his personality, whatever you like to call it — does not reside in his kidneys or liver, or even in his heart or eyes. And any scientist is welcome to all those parts of me for any purpose whatsoever that might conceivably benefit any member of my own species, or any other.

WHO'LL COME AND EAT
MY STARLINGS?

Can anybody tell me, do the Italians eat starlings? I've heard, from friends and relations who've travelled in Italy, that in Italian markets you see small birds killed and skewered for sale. All migrant birds, which they've caught, to the disgust of most English people. But I want to find somebody who eats starlings.

It never seemed so bad to me — to kill things if you're going to eat them rather than just doing it wantonly. Some years ago, I remember reading that big flocks of starlings were doing damage to high buildings in London. They nested on them, they made mess on them and did considerable damage, and various methods were tried out against them. The surfaces of roofs were covered with slippery oil so that the starlings couldn't settle; the first time they tried to, they skidded down the roofs and off at the eaves. But the starlings outwitted the authorities, and they bombed the roofs from high above with their dung, until it had built up to such an extent that, dried off, they could land on it and nest in the eaves as they had originally wanted. I laughed at the time. Nice to think of a flock of starlings defeating all the experts on high buildings in London. It's nice until the starlings turn their attention to you.

It started last year — a large number of them nested on three sides of my house, keeping away the swallows that used to nest there and were no trouble to anybody. In the middle of the summer, when I thought their nests were empty, I called in the carpenter, to block up the spaces between the rafters, and take down the nests, to drive the starlings away. After an hour the carpenter came down from his ladder and said in rather an embarrassed way, 'I know you'll think I'm a great big softie, but I can't do it. They've still got young ones in the nest.'

'All right then, come back in the winter.'

He came back in the winter; he blocked up all the holes and put fine mesh netting round the seat of the rafters so they couldn't get in, with one exception which was outside my bedroom window. 'I'm sorry, I can't do that bit,' he said, 'at least not without some very complicated scaffolding, but they weren't nesting there last year.'

And from early this spring, I've been woken at first light by

chattering and quarrelling starlings in great numbers. All the ones that used to nest on the other three sides of the house have concentrated there, immediately above my window. To start with I felt fairly charitable towards them, as to all birds. And then, when it started to get light earlier, and they started their quarrelling at five in the morning, I began to think, 'Why the hell do they have to use my house? Why can't they build houses of their own in the trees, like other birds? They're just lazy, idle, good-for-nothing creatures.'

I nearly got somebody to shoot all the adults, but I didn't like the idea of the starving babies in their nests, so I thought we'd wait until they had all flown, and get them shot. Then somebody told me, 'Don't forget that they don't just hatch out one lot a year, they'll keep on all summer now. You've got 'em for good.'

Meantime, they're doing on my windows what they used to do on the roofs in London, and they're becoming filthier and filthier, and for the same reason that the carpenter couldn't get at that point to net in the rafter seat, the window cleaner can't get up there either. And I'm ashamed that anybody should see my bedroom with its filthy windows.

Even while I'm writing this, I've discovered they're nesting in the chimney as well. So I can't even have a fire if the weather turns cold. I wouldn't like the idea of burning them alive in their nests. I suppose I shall have to put a cap on the chimney in the summertime, but I'm sure they'll be back again next year.

And then, this morning, this thought occurred to me. If the Italians like eating small birds, it wouldn't seem half so bad if all the starlings, young and old, were eaten. Could I, perhaps, find some enthusiastic Italian bird-catchers to come and catch all the starlings that nest in my house, all their young, the whole bloomin' tribe? Thereby maybe saving some lives of migrant birds passing over Italy. But do they eat them? Somebody tell me.

How the Sanitary Inspector Put
a Stop to Organic Farming

Organic farming is in the news. Farming papers tell me that if I grew organic crops, I would get more money for what I grew and wouldn't lose much in the way of yield. I suspect that, like other theories, there is quite a lot in it but that it doesn't represent the whole truth.

Some chemicals need other chemicals to counteract their side-effects. Some don't seem to work at all. Just at this moment there are about one thousand pigeons feeding on our rape crop, notwithstanding the fact that it was treated, at considerable expense, with a chemical that was supposed to keep them away. They seem to relish it. Some people's views seem to be coloured by childhood stories of the mad scientist who risks the whole world with his experiments. Scientists, witch-doctors, witches, they're all the same sort of villains.

Until the middle of the last century, all farming in this country was, in effect, organic farming. Farmers tried to return to their land, as much as possible, what they had taken out of it, and for hundreds of years the fertility of the land was reasonably maintained by that method; although there was in fact a steady drain of fertility over the centuries, so small that nobody really noticed. The by-products of crops were all fed to livestock and returned to the land.

The food that human beings ate mostly went back to the land by way of the night soil cart. Thousands of tons of human waste was brought out of London and spread on the farms of Hertfordshire, because that county was near London; so it gained a reputation as one of the best farmed counties in Britain. Around the smaller towns every bit of human waste and household waste went back on to the nearest farm. The beautiful deep, black soil in the gardens of most old country cottages was built up by many years of digging-in the contents of the earth closet.

So why did it all change? What went wrong so suddenly? It wasn't greedy farmers wanting to make more profits. It wasn't even ambitious chemists manufacturing chemicals which they thought would increase crop yields. It was the Public Health Acts, and the sanitary inspector, that sounded the death knell of organic farming in Britain.

In the 1860s there was a cholera epidemic in the town of Chesham. As a result a sewage system was constructed with all possible speed, and the farms near the town ceased to have the benefit of the waste. So all that manurial value was destroyed in the sewage farm, the resulting water went out into the river, and there was no more cholera — although once or twice some fish died. On a much larger scale, the same thing was happening everywhere else. It was at a time when there was plenty of cheap food coming in from North America grown on the accumulated fertility of thousands of years of the American prairies — cultivation that was ultimately to create dustbowls.

Providentially, at about the same time, gas started to be used in all the towns in Britain, and a by-product was ammonia, which was found to be a useful fertilizer. So the products of the gasworks replaced the product of the chamberpot. Likewise, nitrate came in from Chile and other places in South America, which was the accumulation of hundreds of years of sea birds' dung piling up in the dry climate. Both these things were hailed as artificial manures and were attacked by traditional farmers (though they are not particularly artificial, anyway).

Earth closets in cottage gardens continued much longer, right up until the early years of this century, providing the rich soil that grew vegetables full of traditional goodness to give the children that lived on them healthy red complexions — and probably tapeworms as well.

Now it's all gone and people are crying out for its return without exactly knowing what they are crying for.

A Scottish farming friend told me a story which rather illustrates the whole point. Next to his father's farm there was a hardworking farmer who spent his whole life trying to improve his small, poor farm. When he had nothing else to do he would go out day after day picking up the stones to improve his farm. Half his life had been spent picking up stones. One day my friend's father stopped to talk to him: 'I see you're still picking stones?' He said, 'Yes, I was thinking to myself the other day, if all those millions of people in Glasgow would just come out here at the weekend and each of them would pick up a stone and put it in his pocket and each of them would have a shit, I should have the best farm in the whole of Scotland.' That's about the way it is.

Every new scientific thing that comes out, every new chemical, whether manure or spray, gets abused to start with, and used too much, and then people find its limitations and either stop using it or limit its use. But it is chemicals and chemical farming which has given the world a surplus of food instead of a shortage. A sudden return to organic farming would quickly take us back to shortages.

Now there is hope that science will produce new methods of improving crops without dangerous chemicals, Genetic engineerng will give the botanists a chance to breed new crops that fix their own nitrate from the air and make better use of the other chemicals in the soil. Just like some crops already do. So don't treat the botanist who goes in for genetic engineering as a mad witch-doctor, especially as it will probably be the botanist in the end who produces the plants to grow the fuel oil we shall need when everything else runs out.

'HAGBERG NO GOOD . . .'

It was an appalling harvest. When all should have been safely gathered in by modern methods, half our corn was still standing in the fields spoiling. And it looked so good. In the June it had never looked better. We'd done it right for once: enough but not too much of the sprays, enough but not too much of the fertilizers. Everything standing and looking good.

It wasn't just a question of the quantity being less. It was the quality which was worrying us now. In years gone by, we judged the quality by smell and taste and feel and, however bad it was, you always hoped you would find a buyer who had temporarily lost his sense of taste and smell and who, in an unobservant mood, would give you a decent price for your inferior wheat. I don't suppose it happened very often, but you had a vague hope.

Nowadays, all hope is gone. All because of this man Hagberg — because he codified with a scientific test all the things we used to do with our senses, and all the things the millers used to do with theirs.

Nowadays they do a test on your wheat and they would say, almost inevitably that year, 'Hagberg no good, no good for milling, much reduced price for animal feed.'

When things go wrong the only consolation one can get — which is really not very kindly motivated — is to look at other people, and see that they are doing worse. Knowing that your neighbours are looking at you in the same way. 'That crop was laid because the silly fool gave too much fertilizer.' 'That crop sprouted, perhaps because it should have been harvested a few days earlier.' Some of it with a little hypocrisy. 'Poor old Tom, it's a pity he got kidded by those salesmen to grow that new variety of wheat, Moulins, with such an attractive name, which has turned out in a sunless summer to yield almost not at all.' We didn't fall for that one; we were probably just lucky, but it always seems that it may have been one's own virtue. This has gone on for ever.

The plain fact is that when, like farmers, you are in competition with the elements and with market conditions, neither of which you have much control over, the only competition that you can control is one of your own competence in doing the job, and the only way to boost your own self-confidence in that is to see other people's faults — conscious all the time that they are seeing yours. It is most encouraging if your mistakes are all well away from the public roads; sometimes I think people take more trouble with the fields that are close to the roads, just to preserve their image.

Mostly, if you make mistakes, you are severely punished. If you take that day off when you ought to be sowing, somehow the weather always turns against you, so instead of being one day late, you are two or three weeks late. The same with your hay, the same with your harvest.

I remember years ago, when a wealthy Daddy bought a local farm for his son, newly marrying a most attractive wife, he built a new bungalow for them and set them up. They went into the farm in the winter and in the spring they were still honeymooning, so they didn't drill their barley in March and April as we, the virtuous, all did. They left it and did it in May, and we said, it won't be any good, it never is around here if you drill as late as that. But that year May was wet and early June was wet, and his barley grew and prospered splendidly. August was wet as well when ours was ready, and it wasn't very good. His wasn't ready till September and the weather turned and was fine and beautiful and when he came back from the long summer holiday we didn't think he should have had — although I don't blame him, remembering what his wife looked like — he combined his barley in perfect condition and probably sold it at a good price.

Somehow it seemed wrong. Providence wasn't being fair. The virtuous had been punished and the idle and improvident had been rewarded. But it didn't last. The next year he behaved in the same way and nature behaved in its normal way and he was soon out of the farm. Perhaps he didn't need to work, perhaps Daddy was wealthy enough for that.

All those times were in the days when we trusted our senses — the smell, the feel, the taste. Now that was all gone. Our wheat was standing dripping in the fields, its quality lost for ever. Mr Hagberg had decreed that all the world should know that it would be no good — that we hadn't got a chance of selling it at any decent price. Miraculously, in a large acreage, we had a tiny bit which Mr Hagberg's test revealed was of a very high quality. That was worth 30 per cent more than any of the other — just think what our harvest might have been without the weather, and without Mr Hagberg, and perhaps with some millers with no sense of taste.

And in the meantime, there was nothing to do but to try to forget that year's harvest and get on with getting ready for the following year's. To do our work as well as we could, feel self-righteous about it, and think that maybe we were doing it better than anybody else and next year perhaps we would be so rewarded. And self-righteously hope that our neighbours wouldn't be kidded by those seedsmen again into growing the wrong varieties. Halfway through September the half of our land that had been harvested was ready for the next year's planting. We really believed we had done it better than we had ever done it before. I wondered if our neighbours passing by thought the same thing. Or that we were quite out of our minds and ought to wait patiently and do it later in the autumn the way it used to be done, and that would have been the way to avoid disaster.

There are so many ways of doing things and they are so often wrong. Hagberg — he's never wrong.

SERVICE

People talk about the increasing number of people employed in what are called 'service industries'. I don't think we are getting more service. It is a fact that in the supermarkets there is a range of supplies that would have been unthinkable half a century ago: fruits and vegetables from all over the world, all the year round, and prepared food of all sorts all ready to use, to say nothing of the innumerable ordinary household requisites in enormous variety. But you've got to go and fetch them. Is that really service?

Foreigners often express amazement that we get our milk delivered on the doorstep; it appears that nobody else in the world does. They look upon it as being out of date — you might as well pick up your milk at the supermarket along with everything else. I think it's the last relic of a society that was, to a much greater extent than now, based on service. Whoever you were, rich or poor, you could if you wished get everything delivered to your door. Everything that you could afford and which was normally available. Bread was regularly delivered; in the towns it was delivered fresh every day, in the villages, several times a week. The grocers and butchers delivered. At the beginning of the week somebody from the grocers' came round from door to door, taking the orders which were then delivered at the end of the week. The local Co-op had several men going round on bicycles to the different villages, collecting peoples' orders, and the large horse-van came round on Fridays and Saturdays and delivered what they had ordered. In the really remote places the van one week took the order for the next week, but all delivered to your door, and the private grocers did the same.

Of course people went shopping as well, but only when they wanted, they didn't have to rush home from work, queue up with a trolley in a supermarket and pay for a car park, and get everything they needed for a week or two. The present system may be more efficient, but it does not represent service.

I remember very clearly, in the 1920s, the man from the local grocers' in Chesham, Whiteman's Stores, calling round. At the time my mother had a maid who was trying to be very lady-like and precise in her language. She came in one day and said to my mother, 'That

Mr Birch is at the back door, fornicating for orders.' To this day, I can't work out what word she thought she was using!

There were also simple forms of mobile shops. There was a butcher from Bovingdon who came round Whelpley Hill, Ley Hill and the other villages once a week with a fairly comprehensive supply of meat in his cart, which he could give you at the door, weighing off exactly what you wanted. His overheads were low and I very much doubt if the prices, relative to other things, were anywhere near as high as they are now. Packaging and freezer cabinets have to be paid for.

Earlier on, on an even simpler sort of basis, there were various specialized traders working from horses and carts. There was Mr Brownsell who dealt simply in eggs and tea. He was what was known as a 'higgler'; he went round the villages, a different one each day of the week, such as Ley Hill one day, Lee Common the next, picking up eggs from regular suppliers, and perhaps chickens as well, and selling them tea. As far as I am aware, nothing else. And when he got back to Chesham he sold the eggs and the chickens to shopkeepers and bought more tea wholesale. A very simple and straightforward form of trading — almost, but not quite, barter.

And because of the large numbers of ordinary people who kept chickens and rabbits, and small livestock of all sorts, there were no less than four corn chandlers in Chesham to service them. Corn chandlers are something that have disappeared off the face of the earth. Their shops were marvellously artistic creations. Their windows were piled up with grain of different sorts, forming intricate patterns: dark, almost red maize, lighter-coloured barley, brown wheat — all sorts of grain piled up in artistic geometric patterns. When you went in for something for your poultry or your rabbits they didn't, of course, serve you from the window and disturb it, it was too much a permanent work of art; they served you from the bins behind, which contained quantities of all the things exhibited in the window.

These corn chandlers also ran mobile services around the villages; each one of them went out every day of the week with a small dray and quantities of grain on board to sell to poultry- and rabbit-keepers in the villages, and pig-keepers as well, and maybe to take orders for larger quantities which they would deliver the following week: pig food and bran and dog biscuits and everything of that nature. All this and the big element of service combined, has disappeared from the face of the earth. I knew, particularly, one of these, Teddy Burgess, because he called on us with supplies for the poultry which were kept here even before my father had a farm. I also saw him when I was at school at Chartridge because he went that way once a week and I remember he boosted my ego no end by recognizing me and calling me 'Mr. Harman'. Boosted the ego of a small nine-year-old boy quite enormously.

These large numbers of suppliers all provided a service, all over the countryside, at intervals appropriate to their situation, obviously long intervals if they were very isolated, but always a service of some sort to everybody at their door. Travelling greengrocers, occasionally a travelling fishmonger, everything of that sort, and what is more, the small shop keepers in the town provided much more genuine service than anybody provides now. Bakers would even cook people's Sunday lunch for them; nowadays an inconceivable service.

At the very bottom level of this door-to-door service was the man who took the rubbish away — no dustman, no municipal dustman, privatized or otherwise but a number of rag-and-bone men who could make use of almost everything you had — the rest was burnt. The one I knew best was Abel Southam. He lived in Chesham and went out every day of the week to a different village with his little trolley and came back loaded with bits and pieces which he knew where to sell — rags, bones, old bits of metal. Of course that was going on in all the big cities of Britain as well. Abel was a bit different in a way, he must have been a very lonely man, by himself all the while whatever the weather. But I knew him quite well and I remember in 1946 I had pneumonia and when I had recovered I met him in the road again and he asked me where I'd been. I told him I'd had pneumonia, and he said, 'I remember having that once. I was coming home from Lee Common one terrible cold, wintry night, and by mistake I opened my mouth and I felt something come in. It must have been the pneumonia germ 'cos I was terrible ill the next day and took weeks to recover. It must have been that pneumonia germ I felt going in.' Wouldn't it be nice if infection and medical science was as simple as that? You could actually feel the germs entering you so you would know when to commence treatment.

All in all, we have a fuller life; we have tropical fruit, we have green peas all the year round (but they don't ever taste as good as they used to when they first came in, in June), but we don't get the service that we used to get, not the genuine service.

CHRISTMAS HAMPERS AND
EMBALMED BUTLERS

Lord Bittisham's mansion is in the Home Counties; it stands in a beautiful park with large, mature trees and a lake, originally laid out in the 18th century in the style of Capability Brown. The actual mansion was built much later. His ancestor, who had made money in the City during the Napoleonic Wars, bought the park with its quite small Queen Anne house, which he didn't consider sufficiently imposing; he tore down the house and built a much larger, grander one. A succession of marriages of the eldest son to the daughters of successful industrialists and bankers made them, by the beginning of the 20th century, one of the wealthiest families in the land.

The town, from which he took his title, was about three miles away. Near to the house was a small village, of about twenty houses and a church, but no pub. His Lordship had never allowed a pub in the village, but it didn't matter much because the occupants of the cottages were almost all retired servants of the house, retired butlers, gardeners, grooms. And a succession of his Lordship's butlers had a good sideline; selling the occupant's liquor from his Lordship's cellar at very reasonable prices.

There were one or two younger people living in the cottages. Unkind people in the countryside around said they were getting a pension because their fathers, who had been butlers of the house, were upstairs in one of the bedrooms, embalmed and dead, but not yet buried and therefore entitled to a pension.

After the First World War the family fortunes had started to decline a bit. They had made unsuccessful speculations on the Stock Exchange, and suffered during the Depression of the 'twenties, but had survived and maintained their standard of life by selling property they owned in London, principally Ballinger Square — the family name was Ballinger. The first peer, Henry Ballinger, had, amongst other assets, considerable estates in London itself which, over the years, had become worth a very large amount of money.

Right up to the Second World War, life on the estate went on as it had always done. The butler sold his master's liquor unnoticed; and the cook got commission out of the grocer who delivered, and from the fishmonger and baker — she made it quite clear to them that unless she got something, they would not supply the house. Gibb, the head gardener, got kick-backs from nurserymen, and from the suppliers of fertilizers and other garden requisites. The groom was paid regularly by the local corn merchant in return for buying rather more oats than the horses could ever eat. He therefore got his kick-back and had a bit for sale as well. It was a little more difficult for the two chauffeurs. They hadn't been in the business so long, and the most they could hope for was, when they filled the cars up with petrol, if none of the family were on board, to get the garage to give them part of the proceeds and put less petrol in. So everybody was very happy and the family were none the wiser about what was going on.

This was in the days of the fifth Baron who, by the end of the Second World War, was quite elderly and had emigrated to East Africa where he bought an estate, leaving his son to come out of the army and pick up the business at home. The Honourable James Ballinger was an earnest young man, wishing to do right by everybody. He'd had a distinguished career in the war, come back and realized that it would be difficult to put things together again as they'd been in his father's time.

The house had been used by the Forces for five years; the staff had gone into temporary jobs where they hadn't had all the advantages they had formerly enjoyed. But they had their expectations: the Honourable James would come back and re-establish everything as it was. All through the war the family had been paying the pensions of the retired staff living in the village. Paying their rates for them, even keeping up the Christmas hampers, though not on the grand scale of the past.

The Honourable James examined his list of tenants with the help of Mackintosh, the elderly Scots agent, who'd been seriously fiddling the books for many years. He noticed that there were several people of extraordinarily great age living in the cottages, and asked Mackintosh about them. There was no reply, so the Honourable James made enquiries himself. He wasn't shown into any of the upper rooms in the cottages, but there followed a series of hasty funerals for some very aged people.

James soon realized that there was no hope of his going back to the lifestyle of his father. Too much money had been taken out of the estate, and wages had risen so high that such a staff would cost a huge sum of money. It was 1946. He called all the staff together and made an apologetic statement: 'You have all served my family loyally for very many years; indeed, some of you are descendants of staff who have served my family for generations. But, I'm afraid the world has changed; I shall have to sell up the estate and live on a more modest scale.'

The reception to this news was one of horror. They had all been expecting to go back to normality, back to the easy life with its lucrative sidelines. Their families had always supported the family in its politics. In Victorian times the family had been Liberals, so the estate workers had been Liberals. When later, over the Irish question, they had joined the Tories, the staff followed suit. They had gone to the meetings held in the village and had cheered his Lordship. Suddenly their idea of what was right and proper had been shattered. The family had let them down, and they would be revenged. But how?

By 1950, when a general election was called and the Honourable James selected as a Conservative candidate — in another constituency — all the former staff joined the local Labour Party. They were led by Gibb, the former head gardener, who had suddenly discovered Radical traditions within his own family, and who acted as a focus for everyone else to show their disapproval of the decay of the old order.

And so the estate was duly broken up; the mansion becoming the headquarters of an industrial company, the cottages in the village, as they became vacant, being sold off. But James kept most of the park, and its lake. He retained with it a yearning for the gentle lifestyle he could remember as a boy and, later, as a young man. However, he had begun to suspect that those polite and deferential servants who had been so kind to him when he was young were not exactly as they seemed.

Then, some years later, in 1970, he decided to come back, to try and live near the ancestral village, even if he could no longer live in the mansion itself. He applied for planning permission to build a large — but not excessive — house in the remainder of the park. Now nobody was allowed to do that sort of thing, but it was different with him. The villagers, mostly former servants, petitioned that he be allowed to build his home, so that the family could come back. Their socialism forgotten, they decided that the old days of huge hampers and profitable sidelines was the best life. And, maybe one day, they might even get back to the situation where, when they themselves died, their families could embalm them and keep them upstairs so that they could continue to enjoy their pensions.

THE WILL

Reading the will would, of course, be just a formality. Mabel Jackson knew exactly what was in it. She had not witnessed it because, as the main beneficiary, indeed the sole beneficiary, she was not allowed to. But, she had insisted on Albert making it very many years ago when they had gone down together with their friends, George and Alice Atkins to the bank, and it had all been signed and sealed in front of the Manager of Barclays Bank who would be the executors.

The will quite simply said, 'I leave everything to my widow, Mabel,' all of course wrapped up in the proper legal language. Albert had not appeared to be a very business-like man and everyone had managed him all his life, especially Mabel. She had always told him how much more efficient their friends, the Atkins were. He rarely showed signs of resentment. All the money he made had been carefully banked. There was bound to be a tidy sum there. In fact, she had from time to time checked it up.

She had just been shown into the Manager's office and offered the routine condolences, when his phone rang. It was a Mr Perks from the National Westminster who wished to speak to him: 'I have here a will of your client, Albert Jackson, just deceased, which I think may possibly post-date any will you might have.' This somewhat startled the Manager, who then had to tell Mrs Jackson and the Atkins, that although he would read the will, there might well be another, and that he would send one of his clerks down the road to collect the envelope from the other bank. He arranged for one of his staff to get them a cup of tea and, within ten minutes, one of his assistants came in bearing a large envelope from the National Westminster Bank.

When it was opened it contained a will made only five years before, long after the other will, and duly witnessed by two members of the staff of the other bank. The Manager started reading: 'I leave everything I have to my widow, Mabel, who has stood by me all these years, except for two other bequests: One thousand pounds to our friend George Atkins, for taking Mabel off my hands on one or two occasions when she was being tiresome. I don't resent it in the least but I knew perfectly well what was going on, and this is an acknowledgement of my appreciation. Sometimes I have even thought that our son, Tom, looked a bit more like you, George, than me.'

There was a horrified silence in the room and Mrs Atkins looked at her husband furiously and said, 'What does this mean, George? And, as for you, Mabel Jackson!'

'I know nothing about it' George said. 'I never had anything to do with her, except when you were there.'

'Well, there was a lot of occasions when I was off at the Womens' Institute and things like that and you must have gone and slipped out. Plenty of opportunities.'

'Well, we won't take the money anyway,' George said.

'That's hardly the point, is it?'

With that the Manager said flatly, 'I'm sorry but I haven't finished yet.' He went on 'Two thousand pounds to Alice Atkins for that one night back in 1955 when my wife was staying away with her sister and George was off buying sheep in Scotland — it was well worth it.'

Immediately, of course, Alice Jackson flushed even more deeply and became thoroughly flustered: 'It is quite untrue; I never went anywhere near him when you were away — you know I wouldn't have done that, Mabel.'

By now, everybody was thoroughly suspicious. They were all declaring loudly that they wouldn't take the money anyway and that there was nothing in any of it. Did anybody really believe their denials?

After all those years and years when everybody had sat round saying what a bad businessman he was, telling him how to look after his money, having to make wills and things like that, one thing was clear: Albert had had his revenge.

WHERE HAVE ALL THE
FLOWERS GONE?

It used to be such a quiet place. On Saturday afternoons, if I went outside my front door, I could hear the crowds in the nearest town three miles away, at a football match, cheering on Chesham United. Of course, there isn't a crowd now anyway, because people don't go to local football matches. They go to the big league matches in London and Watford and Luton, but then they supported the local team: I suppose they couldn't afford to travel, and local things meant so much more in those days. But now even if there was a crowd there, I wouldn't hear it. The noise of the planes and the noise of lorries and the noise of the traffic in the town would drown it all.

Sometimes, then, I could even hear in the other direction an occasional outburst of noise from the village football ground a mile and a half away. The village team had the reputation of getting angry and fighting, so every now and then you could hear outbursts of shouting. I don't know whether there is a village football team any more; if there is, they certainly don't fight. Perhaps some of them go to big league games and create trouble there, for all I know.

Because it was so quiet, you knew what your neighbours were doing. You heard the hum of the thrashing machine when they were thrashing; or the juddering of the mower when they were mowing; or the singing of ring rolls in the spring on the hard, stony ground. And above all you heard the birds, much more than now. Some of the things that conservationists protest about aren't true, but one is, there are far fewer birds. It isn't just that so many of the hedgerows in which they live have been done away with; it is that the remaining hedges are kept close cut, limiting the amount of refuge open to them, and limiting the production of berries for their winter feed.

The worst offenders in these matters are the county councils who habitually trim the roadside hedges which were the home, particularly, of the yellow-hammers, during the nesting season. And how many nests of young birds their machines destroy, nobody can possibly tell. Farmers don't cut their hedges generally in the nesting season.

The world was a beautiful place, as well as quiet, at the bottom of the agricultural depression. I don't know, but I think it was probably more beautiful then than it had ever been since the orginal clearance of the forest many centuries ago. Neglect of good farming means there are plenty of weeds; and weeds on the whole are wild flowers. I expect that in the 18th century, during the great farming revolution, they were all pulled out by hand, but then later, in the middle of the last century when agriculture went into decay, there wasn't enough labour left to do that and weeds multiplied. So that in the 1920s and 1930s, the fields were bright with wild flowers of all sorts. A regular sequence of changing colours. In the end of May, the fields of corn all yellow with charlock, generally standing higher than the corn, and bright yellow. Charlock has been entirely destroyed by modern farming methods, by sprays. There are yellow fields now, but they are fields of rape, a darker, denser yellow, and there by design and not by accident.

While the arable fields were yellow, the meadows were white with big dog-daisies, and after that they were dark yellow with buttercups, or sometimes both together; patches of white and patches of yellow. And in amongst them, if you looked, were little purple orchids. The arable fields, almost as soon as the charlock flowers had fallen off, and had ceased to be yellow, suddenly became bright scarlet with poppies. There are still fields that are bright scarlet with poppies, but not very many, just where the farmers have failed to clear them, failed to kill them. And the poppy is a most resolute plant; its seed appears to live forever and as soon as the farmer drops his guard, the fields become red again. But then they all used to become red.

The big, sprawling hedges were also a symbol of agricultural depression because in the 18th century they would have been kept carefully trimmed and laid, when the charlock and poppies would have been pulled out by hand. But there hadn't been enough labour on the farms since, and the hedges had spread themselves everywhere, and grown out of control, and they too went through their succession of colour changes.

Quite early in the spring, big, white patches of blackthorn appeared, associated in people's minds always with a cold snap, the so-called 'blackthorn winter'; no genuine association. Soon after that, the may on the hawthorn trees. There's still a fair bit of that about, but mostly on the edges of towns, where new quickthorn hedges have been planted and allowed to grow. Not long after the last hawthorn petals had fallen, the hedges were festooned with honeysuckle and that lasted a long time, overlapping the season when there were wild roses everywhere; some pink, some white. And then, as soon as they had gone, the honeysuckle still lingering on, bramble flowers hanging off the branches and promising the fruit for the autumn. By September, big, dark purplish-blue patches where the blackthorn had been, and blackberries where the bramble flowers were. And everywhere else, red berries; dark-red berries on the may trees; big, bright-red berries where the roses has been; and round, red berries of innumerable climbing plants one had hardly noticed.

And over it all, great drifts of what looked like almost human hair. Old man's beard, or Daddyman's beard as it was more commonly called in Buckinghamshire; one hadn't even noticed its flower in season because it was so green and inconspicuous. You notice it in the winter all right — big strands and tresses of it. Of course there are still berries in the autumn but they seem to disappear very quickly, although there are far fewer birds. I suppose in proportion to the number of birds there are even fewer berries. There were so many berries all those years ago that they seemed to hang on the whole winter. Perhaps in the end there was nothing left but the holly berries — but they were there, as a sort of final reserve for the bird population, left alone because of the prickles on the leaves, but taken in the end. Now they disappear very quickly.

And then, for a brief period, there is an infinite variety of colours in the hedge itself. In Buckinghamshire there's a lot of brown, from the nut hazel, whose leaves, when the nuts are ripe, go a rather dull and inconspicuous brown. But here and there are patches of maple, brilliant yellow for a short period, the leaves when they fall off eagerly gobbled up by any passing cow; and in the bottom of the hedge, the dog-wood going deep purplish-red for a brief period before the leaves fall off. The occasional beech retaining its leaves all winter, with its warm brown colour. Funny how the beech, if it is small and kept short, retains its leaves, but as soon as it grows into a tree all the leaves fall off.

All these things one noticed when one was walking and saw quite casually because the pace of life was slower. They stick in my mind from various occasions, especially walking cows home from farm sales. One was July, all the way from Ballinger with an enormous variety of hedges on the way — all the things I've described and more. You couldn't drive a cow from Ballinger now — too much traffic about — too many suburban houses with their gates open and angry men in the gardens who would roar at your cow if she looked at them and would send her speeding on her way at a pace you couldn't keep up with.

Bringing another cow back from the bottom end of Chesham, I remember a lane with lots of elderberry bushes, not noted so much on the Lee Common journey. Large trusses of small, white flowers in the early summer; replaced by deep purple berries in the autumn, edible berries which nobody in England bothers to eat, they just occasionally make them into wine. And then, the cow called Moonshine, named after a farm where she was born at Flaunden. I remember bringing her back, straight across the middle of a common, with gorse bushes that still remain, but with raspberries which have all gone. Everybody used to go and pick the raspberries in those days.

And the changing colours of the fields are irrevocably linked in my mind to the wartime period when I had to sleep out in the middle of a field at night on watch in a small dug-out, playing at soldiers in the Home Guard. I was there at first light. Larks singing in the sky. I think they are still there, because they, after all, nest in the open and don't need hedges. But I don't hear them because I am not up in time, nor do I believe is anybody else. And then, the whole world for one week or two was yellow, brilliant yellow and, with the dew on the ground, there was a faint, sweet smell of charlock, not altogether pleasant. Then after that, the whole world turned red with poppies which smelt not at all unless you picked them, and then rather nasty. And as the summer wore on, everything turned to gold and back to brown in the autumn.

I don't know whether another agricultural depression would return all this beauty to the countryside, I rather doubt it on the whole. The poppies would multiply in the fields and the charlock would, probably, return because any single plant produces a thousand the following year if left to itself. But the hedges, those that are not gone, are mostly by the roadside, and your urban motorist, so concerned with what the farmers have done to the countryside, would shout loudly if the council allowed the hedges to grow and interrupt his view of the road. He would insist upon the hedges being cut and the flowers and birds destroyed.

In spite of it all, some odd things survive. The wild gooseberry bush growing in a hedge with its very small, hairy fruit is in the same place beside the lane that it was in when I saw it as a very small child. I can remember Annie Waller pushing me along in a pushcart, picking the gooseberries. It is still there, it has survived all the cutting and trimming. And, a little farther on there's a spindle berry bush. These bushes were always there, as a comparative rarity — maybe one per mile of roadside hedge — but the one I first saw is still there: dark green and rather anonymous all summer (its name is Euonymous) but bright pink in the winter, with berries shaped like bishops' caps, as our Austrian au pair girl once described it. So some things have survived more strongly than one might expect, particularly things that always were quite uncommon.

Other plants adapt to civilization and modernization very quickly. There are more primroses and cowslips on railway embankments than ever there are on farms. And if the highway authority would just forget its obsession with frequent cutting of everything within sight, the motorway verges would rapidly become a refuge for all the rare sorts of wild flowers, besides being covered with masses of common things like dog-daisies.